Loose Girl

Loose Girl

Some girls are anorexic.
Others choose alcohol or drugs.
I chose sex.

Kerry Cohen

EBURY
PRESS

This book is a work of nonfiction. I have changed most names and identifying details. I have also, at times, combined certain characters to allow for narrative sense. I have tried to recount the circumstances as best I remember them, but memory can be a faulty device. Facts are important, but I believe that even more important than the facts is truth. I trusted truth to guide me as I wrote. Jack Kerouac once said, "Everything I wrote was true because I believed what I saw." So it is for this book.

7 9 10 8

Published in 2008 by Ebury Press, an imprint of Ebury Publishing
A Random House Group Company
First Published in the USA by Hyperion in 2008

The Random House Group Limited Reg. No. 954009

Addresses for companies within the Random House Group can be found at www.randomhouse.co.uk

A CIP catalogue record for this book is available from the British Library

The Random House Group Limited supports The Forest Stewardship Council (FSC), the leading international forest certification organisation. All our titles that are printed on Greenpeace approved FSC certified paper carry the FSC logo. Our paper procurement policy can be found at www.rbooks.co.uk/environment

Printed in the UK by CPI Antony Rowe, Chippenham, Wiltshire

ISBN 9780091922719

To buy books by your favourite authors and register for offers visit www.rbooks.co.uk

Everything always, now, for E. and G.

Acknowledgments

BECAUSE THIS BOOK was an effort that spanned a full decade, the people I have to thank for its creation are almost innumerable. But I will do my best.

The seed for *Loose Girl* began in 1996, long before I had lived out its last page. My teachers at the time, especially Garrett Hongo, Ehud Havazelet, and Chang-rae Lee, offered the encouragement, guidance, and intellectual understanding of my work to carry with me long after I left their classrooms. Sally Tisdale saw a very early draft of the first chapter at a workshop and said simply, "Keep writing." Patricia Benesh and Rebecca Grabill offered generous, thoughtful direction and critique as first readers of the book. These gifted writers and mentors could not have known how much their words riveted, inspired, and challenged me.

The work of Naomi Wolf, Susan Bordo, Judith Butler, Audre Lorde, Mary Pipher, Lyn Mikel Brown and Carol Gilligan, Joan Jacobs Brumberg, and Ariel Levy helped me think through the problem I was trying to pinpoint in my

7

story. Likewise, Marya Hornbacher's *Wasted*, Elizabeth Wurtzel's *Prozac Nation*, Lucy Grealy's *Autobiography of a Face*, and Koren Zailckas's *Smashed* set a precedent for the kind of story I wanted to tell and inspired me to keep pushing myself to do so.

My agent, Ethan Ellenberg, kindly warned me about the repercussions of exposing myself with such a personal story. Only a person thinking above all else about my happiness would even consider this, and Ethan has showed himself to be that person again and again. I also owe Ethan tremendous gratitude for getting the book into Brenda Copeland's hands. Brenda loved, nurtured, and understood my story as though it were her own child. After nailing a particularly difficult scene together, Brenda wrote me, "Truly, this is why I love my job. Moments like these." What more could an author want in her editor? Brilliance? Vision? Well, she has those, too. Thanks to all the wonderful people at Hyperion – particularly Kathleen Carr, Rachelle Mandik, Robert S. Miller, Michelle Ishay, Navorn Johnson, Allison McGeehon, and Ellen Archer – who have cared enough about this book to tend to it and me with care.

Thanks, as well, to Charlotte Cole at Ebury Press in the UK for her support and good work, and for kindly answering all my obnoxious questions.

Thanks to Terri Brooks-Hernandez, Bevin Cahill, and my many other supportive and loving friends throughout the years. Tommy Mang, my first and only best friend-boy, I owe you much and miss you. Thanks also to Nadine Hamester who cared for my boys while I wrote. And to N.L., who remains in my heart, and to C.

Thanks to the many girls who shared their stories with me over the years. I hope my words then and now have made them and so many others like them feel less alone.

Tremendous gratitude to my father and mother, and to S.B. who made me feel loved when I most needed it. I hope my late grandparents know how much their generosity and kindness sustained and encouraged me. Thank you, Tyler Cohen, my fellow survivor, for never faltering in your love for me.

Thanks to Cat Power, Richard Buckner, Uncle Tupelo, Josh Ritter, Wilco, and Gillian Welch, who provided me with the mood for my story. And since I'm thanking people here, thanks for the likes of Adrian Grenier, Leonardo DiCaprio, Emile Hirsch, Matt Dillon, and Jemaine Clement of the Flight of the Conchords. I may be married now, but I'm not dead.

Love and gratitude to Michael, who has been a support and a friend in more ways than I can list here. Most of all, I thank Ezra and Griffin, who inspired me to write constantly since their births, who have taught me to love fully and with my whole self, and who I hope will forgive me someday for writing a book for all their friends to read about their mother's sex life.

"Boys. Yes, boys come next. After the blood come the boys."

—Margaret White in Stephen King's *Carrie*

Introduction

IN THE DARKNESS, he touches me, his long, strong fingers moving across the surface of my skin, his breath hot and real near my ear. He kisses tenderly, my ear, my neck, my mouth. Slides my shirt over my head, the movement choreographed with his breath. Then his fingers on the button of my jeans, the hesitation. *Will she let me do this?* he must be wondering. And my wordless answer, a movement of the hips. *Yes, yes, always yes.* He slips off the jeans, the underwear, and then on top of me, his solid body, the weight of him, his movement, all so real, all so *there*. It doesn't matter who he is. There are so many of them. Him. Me. Our movement together. Proof, I think again and again, of being worthwhile. Proof of being loved.

❖ ❖ ❖

I SLEPT WITH close to forty boys and men before I figured out doing so was not serving me well. There were many more with whom I did other sexual acts, like oral sex and petting. To some this may seem like a lot. Others will think it not very many at all. There are girls with lists much longer than mine. In truth, I don't really know the length of my list. After twenty-five I lost count. Sometime in my late twenties I tried to name them all, starting with my first, but I found out quickly I had forgotten a host of names. A few I may not have ever known, and for the larger percentage I didn't know their last names. Still, I sat there, chewing at the end of my pen, the pad of paper before me – *Tom? Tim? Oh, wait, then there was that guy with the dog. And the one who kept talking to me during sex, as though we were just hanging out, what was* his *name?* For a man this might be a pleasant trip down memory lane, counting up his conquests. But for a girl, it's a whole other story. I had let these men inside me, wanting that to make me matter to them. Wanting it to make me matter. Now they were just cross-outs and question marks. At some point, I gave up, disgusted with myself. I crumpled the paper and threw it away.

This is not a list of which I am proud.

Still, it is a telling of my story.

It is the story of any girl who finds herself hurt in some way, who finds herself with pain and then makes a choice to do something about it. Some girls turn to anorexia. Others to alcohol, drugs, cutting, sports, ambition. I chose promiscuity. I am not the only one by far. One of every three girls has had sex by age sixteen, and two out of three by age eighteen. Statistics for 2003 show slightly more girls than boys have had sex before the age of twenty, and casual sex in high school is near equal for boys and girls. A third of teen girls get pregnant before they turn twenty, and 79 percent of these pregnancies are both unintended and to unmarried teens. The younger a girl is when she has her first intercourse, the more likely it is to have been unwanted or not voluntary. Every year about one in four sexually active teens gets an STD. "Friends with benefits" and "hookups" are terms in most contemporary teens' vocabularies. A study released by the American Association of University Women Educational Foundation revealed that of fifty-five girls between the ages of eleven and seventeen, only the eleven-year-olds did not mention pressure to have sex as an issue. But if you eavesdrop on girls in middle school, girls as young as ten and eleven, I guarantee you will hear plenty of talk about blow jobs and sex.

What statistics can't get at are the feelings of uncertainty and confusion that surround a young girl's sexual behavior. They don't get at how easy it is for a girl to use sex for attention. A boy once said to me, "Boys have to put forth real effort to get laid, while all you have to do is stand braless in the wind." It's true. What's easier for a girl than to get noticed for her body? Using my sex appeal was default behavior. To *not* do so would have required more effort. Add to this the fact that I was desperate for attention – any attention – and men's interest in my body was the easiest avenue to being noticed. Of course, I confused their base interest with love. I needed to believe it meant something.

Don't get me wrong. I don't see myself as entirely innocent. My story is also about addiction. Addiction to power, to the attempt to control others through my body. It is about how desperate I was to feel loved, less alone, and how, misguided by all those cultural mixed messages, I tried to fill my need with male attention and sex. How, as with most addictions, I managed to push most everyone away, foiling my greatest intentions. And finally, how I learned to stop.

So I pull that paper full of scratch marks and questions out of the wastebasket, I smooth it out on my desk, and I begin.

PART ONE

A House with No Men

One

I AM ELEVEN the day I begin to understand what it means to be a girl, walking into the next town as I often do, on my way to browse at the pet store or the hobby store, to do something with the endless, hot summer days that seem to stretch on and on. A semi truck, slowing at an intersection, honks. I look up and see a middle-aged man, thirty-five, maybe forty. He is smiling at me, his eyes on my body, dark stubble on his cheeks and chin. "Hello, there," he says, and winks. For the first time, I am aware of my green gym shorts, which stop at the top of my thighs. My white T-shirt feels tight against my training bra. I am just a girl, but I could also be a woman. The man's eyes linger on me, friendly, suggestive. And then he releases the brakes, the truck sighing, and is gone. I stand and watch him go, alert, changed, understanding but not quite understanding.

I think to myself, *That was easy.*

My father moved out recently, another statistic of the 1980s divorce trend, leaving us in a house with no men, just my mother, older sister Tyler, and me. My mother, grief-stricken and frantic, is busy with need. Her need takes up space – so much space there is no room for my own. Sometimes she does physical things with this need, like laying three tons of bluestone to make a patio or ripping out the carpet on the stairs. But more often, her desire weaves through the house like cobwebs. It takes over the house, inch by dirty inch, until there is no air left to breathe that isn't filled with her longing. Some days I come home to find her crouched in a fetal position in the kitchen, her cries loud and terrible, while I stand, my hands open at my sides. Her need is ugly and messy, mixed up with mascara tears and groaning, overflowing and seemingly endless. It pushes me outside, away from her, left to wrestle with my loneliness, and with my own desire that has just started its stirrings.

It is around this time, when I am twelve, that Ashley and Liz, my two closest friends from private school, and I make a plan to meet three boys in New York City. Liz knows one of them, Milo, because he is her mother's friend's son. She knows Milo's mother, a single mom, will be out of town on business Saturday night, leaving him in their apartment on the Upper West Side of Manhattan. Milo is allowed to have a couple of friends stay the night, as long as they promise not to leave the apartment and as long as their parents know they will be there without adult supervision. Liz is a year older than Ashley and me. She has already been to third base with a boy, letting him touch her down there, and because of her expertise with boys we let her take over. According to Liz, we will each tell our parents we are staying at one another's houses for the night. Then we will make our way into the city to Milo's house, where he will wait with two of his friends, Geoff and Dylan.

On Saturday, the three of us get ready at my house.

"Your hair looks good like that," Ashley says after I use the curling iron.

"Those boys aren't going to know what hit them." Liz leans into the mirror, her mouth open as she applies eyeliner. My mother is out with friends, so we are in her bathroom cabinet with her mascara and lipstick and eye shadow.

"We're smokin'," I say, laughing, following Liz's lead. Ashley laughs too.

"Move over, Christie Brinkley," she says.

"Here." Liz bends past me to wipe Ashley's eye. "Your eye shadow's a little smudgy."

My mother owns tons of makeup: Chanel mascara and eye pencils, Yves Saint Laurent and Estée Lauder lipstick, the tubes lined up in rows like little soldiers. No Bonne Bell or Maybelline here. Liz and Ashley are excited that they get to try such expensive brands. There are other things too – tools for tweezing and bleaching and cleansing. So much I don't know about yet when it comes to being a woman. Plenty of mornings I sat on the closed toilet seat and watched my mother stand at this mirror, cleaning, removing, and applying. It struck me as a lot of work to become presentable, but I liked the busyness of it. I liked the idea that I could use these items and become something better than I was. Now it is me at the mirror, applying blush, sucking in my cheeks like I saw her do so many times. We are giggly as we curl our hair and spray it so it feathers. All three of us wear miniskirts and jean jackets. My skirt is denim, and Liz's and Ashley's are black jersey. Liz ties her shirt into a knot so it shows off her stomach. She shows me how to make mine do the same. She does Ashley's, too, but Ashley undoes hers, uncomfortable showing so much skin.

We catch the seven twenty-five bus, which takes us onto Route 9. At the George Washington Bridge we take another bus to the Port Authority at 175th. From there we walk down the long, graffiti-filled corridor to the C train, which we take to West 86th Street. By the time we get to Milo's, it is ten o'clock. The streets are busy with Manhattan nightlife. Girls like us, but much older, walk along Columbus Avenue with lit cigarettes and duck into bars. Men laugh loudly. A couple kisses passionately against a building wall, the man's hand tucked up under the woman's shirt. My friends and I are excited. We are a part of this night, this passion, this potential for deep feeling. Anything can happen, anything at all. We ride the elevator to Milo's floor, our hearts fluttering in our chests.

Milo answers the door, and my heart sinks. I imagined him as much cuter, a boy from the movies. Instead he is short and freckled, like me. In the living room, the boys are watching *Eraserhead*, that bizarre David Lynch film about a man who discovers he has fathered a mutant infant. We sit awkwardly on the couch, clutching our purses on our laps. I can't follow the storyline at all. Instead, the strange images horrify me: the grotesque baby, the woman with swollen cheeks. Eventually, we begin to couple up. Ashley goes off with Geoff, Liz with Dylan, and Milo is left with me. I am used to this, being the one not chosen. It's not that I'm not pretty in my own way. I'm just not notable. A year earlier the boys in my classroom divided us girls into three categories: love, like, and hate. They spent their free reading time huddled around a table and decided which category each of us belonged to. We girls sat at our desks, trying our hardest to read, but really we were all listening hard for our names to come up. Liz, who has blond hair and unfreckled, pale skin was put in the "love" column. When the boys agreed she should be listed there, we all nodded to ourselves. It was no surprise. One sad, awkward girl, a girl who was so tall all the crotches of her tights peeked out below jumpers that were too short, was sequestered to "hate," which again was no surprise. Silently, I hoped they would shock everyone and put me under "love," like Liz. But they didn't. I was clumped with everyone else under "like." Unexceptional and invisible. Not meant to be loved.

Milo takes my hand and we climb the stairs to his small, cluttered bedroom. He presses Play on his tape player, and the Rolling Stones' "Beast of Burden" fills the room. We sit on his bed and, though I have no attraction for him at all, I allow him to kiss me. His tongue is clumsy and unpleasant in my mouth. It is my first kiss, and it isn't at all what I expected. But I stay with it, eager for the experience. He pushes up my shirt and touches my tiny, sensitive nipple with two fingers. Just as he pushes me down on the bed, just as I feel the strange pressure against my leg of his erection through his jeans, there's a knock at the door. I feel a vague relief at being stopped. Milo, though, frustrated at the interruption, opens the door in a huff.

Liz and Ashley stand there, jean jackets on.

"What the fuck?" Milo says.

"We're going." Liz looks at me, ignoring him. Then, to him, "Your friend's an asshole."

"What happened?" I ask.

"Ashley told Geoff no, but he kept pushing."

I look at Ashley who stands beside Liz, her jaw tight. She is clearly upset.

"He wanted to do more than kiss," she says.

I frown, hoping Milo won't say anything about the fact that I just allowed him to put his hands on my breasts. Instead he says, "Why don't you stay and they can go?"

I smile at him appreciatively, but when I look back at my friends, Liz is scowling. "I can't," I say. "But thanks."

24

"Fine," Milo says. I find my jacket and we go to the door. I wait for him to say something as we leave, like he wants to see me again or wants my number. But he just slams the door after us.

"Fuck you," Liz says as we make our way down the hall. "He was always an asshole. I don't know what I was thinking." Ashley and I look at each other and laugh, relieved that it's just the three of us again.

By the time we are outside, it is one thirty a.m. The streets are still lively, but the subway is deserted. Back at the Port Authority, we are conspicuously out of place at this time of night. The buses that travel across the bridge back into New Jersey only come every two hours, so we hang out in the dirty, fluorescent-lit terminal, waiting amid the drug-hungry beggars and the homeless who had found shelter for the night.

Eventually the bus does come, and we ride over the bridge and back toward my house, trying to stay awake. At the top of Closter Dock Road, though, when there is nobody left on the bus but us, the bus stops and the doors exhale open. "Everyone out," the driver says. We sit up, confused. We're going to Harrington Park. But when I ask, the driver informs us that after midnight this is as far as he goes. We try pleading with him to take us anyway, just this once, but he refuses, probably thinking we shouldn't be out there in the first place, three young girls all alone.

So we step down off the bus, and the doors sigh closed. We stand by the side of the road. The air is cool, the night silent. No laughing, no made-up women, no couples and passionate kisses. Just the soft rustling of the leaves as a breeze lifts them. We're ten miles from my house. Ashley starts crying. Liz and I look at each other, trying to determine what to do. Liz sees it first: a few hundred feet down the way is a gas station with the sign "Open 24 hours". We whoop and run toward it, purses banging against our hips. We walk into the office where there are two young men smoking and playing cards. Their eyes light up as we walk in – one, two, three girls, all dressed up in miniskirts. The desk where they sit is metal with a fake wood top. A small, grainy, black-and-white television murmurs on the desk. They clearly weren't expecting anything like this tonight.

"Well, well," the larger one says. He is blond, his face young. "What do we have here?" He glances over at the other one who is dark-haired, skinny, and wearing glasses. That one raises his eyebrows. Liz tells them our story, how we went to the city to meet guys, how they treated us badly, and how now we are stuck here, ten miles from my house. We need a ride home. The clock on the wall reads four a.m. The two men exchange a smile.

"We can't just leave the station," the blond one says. "Right?"

"That's right." The other one nods, his eyes moving from girl to girl.

"You'll have to wait until five," the blond one continues. "That's when we get off."

His face breaks into a smile, and he starts laughing. I can see his teeth are stained yellow. "Get it?" he says to his friend. "That's when we *get off.*" The other one laughs, nodding his head.

The three of us huddle.

"I don't know," Ashley says. She's uncomfortable.

"What else can we do?" Liz frowns.

"They're strange men." Ashley has been warned as we all have: Don't get into cars with strange men.

"C'mere," the blond one says to me when I look back at them. Liz and Ashley widen their eyes at me. Liz giggles.

"What?" I say. Usually Liz is the one getting the attention.

"C'mere," he says again, more insistent.

I bite my lip and sidle up to the desk, unsure what to think.

"How old are you?" he asks, his eyes holding mine.

"Why?" I say.

"Just answer me," he says. "How old?"

This close I can see the age in his face, a weathered darkness that makes him look older than he probably is.

"Sixteen," I lie. I hear Liz giggle again behind me.

"Is that right," he says. He presses his lips together. Clearly he doesn't believe me.

"We all are," Liz says, but he doesn't take his eyes off me.

"You're still jailbait," the other one says. "Right, Tim?"

"That she is." Tim winks at me.

I look down at the desk. Someone has carved into it with a razor: *D loves G.*

"That's gross," Ashley says. She grabs my arm and shoots Tim a look. "We'll be sitting over here until you can take us home." Ashley pulls Liz and me to the other side of the room, and the three of us sit on the ground against the wall. Eventually a car pulls into the station. Loud music streams out the windows, and the boys and girls inside yell to one another. Tim goes out to get them gas. The other one, named Gary, ignores us, keeping his eyes on the grainy television.

"We're not really sixteen," Ashley says suddenly, and Liz smacks her arm.

"No duh," Gary says and snorts.

We look at each other. "How did you know?" I ask.

Gary shrugs. "Sixteen-year-old girls wouldn't be stuck at a gas station in the middle of the night. They'd know somebody who could drive them home."

I feel defensive. "Not every girl."

Gary snorts again. "Oh, yes they do. You girls get whatever you want."

I look down at my legs, which are tucked up under me. It sure doesn't feel like I can have what I want. But I like the idea, stash it away in my mind to come back to later. It is an idea I might need.

Later, Liz and Ashley go around back to the gas station bathroom. I'm alone with Tim. He watches me. I look out the window, pretending I'm not aware of his gaze. I cross my legs and smooth my hair, then fold my arms in front of me.

"You sure are a pretty girl," he says.

I shrug. Nobody's ever called me pretty before.

"You'll be an even prettier woman."

I shift my weight to my left foot and stare at the window. Outside, it is dead quiet, still dark. I watch the shadowy figure of Gary locking one of the tanks.

"Why are you standing all the way over there?" Tim asks.

"Because I want to," I say. I look straight into his eyes. My heart is pounding inside my chest.

"Come over here."

I move toward him, my arms wrapped around my waist.

"Come sit on my lap," he says softly.

"No," I mumble, my throat tightening.

He raises his eyebrows, starting to turn away, looking, perhaps, for one of my friends.

"You'd like that, wouldn't you?" I blurt.

He laughs, a deep, grown-up laugh. "Oh, yes. I would indeed."

That's when Liz and Ashley come back in. I let out my breath, unaware I've been holding it. I look down at my suede boots. I can still feel something like sparks beneath my skin, as though I'm made of electricity. That power again, coursing through me. I'm not attracted to him. In fact, I'm repulsed for the most part. But I like how he saved this talk for me. Not Liz, my pretty friend, not Ashley, who already hates him. Just plain, unremarkable me.

Finally, five o'clock comes. They take their time, locking drawers, sweeping the floor. At five fifteen, the next shift arrives and Tim unlocks the doors of his tan-colored Chevy. We three girls pile into the back. Tim looks back at me from the driver's seat.

"Sit up here with me."

I shake my head. Ashley sets her mouth and looks out the window. She's getting tired of this, of the games and flirtations. We all are. It's been a long night. There's another feeling too: a growing nervousness, the knowledge we're at Tim's will. He can take us anywhere he wants.

"Gary, get in back," Tim says, ignoring me. "Kerry's sitting there."

Gary opens my door, annoyed. "Well?"

I look at Liz.

"Just go, or we'll never get out of here," she says.

Tim smiles when I sit next to him, and I smile back, afraid to upset him. Then he sets a hand on my leg. I look down. His hand is dirty from oil changes, and the skin looks cracked and raw. My muscles go taut. In my head, I start praying: *Just get us home soon.*

"Tell me where to turn," he says, but when I tell him, he drives right past the street. He laughs, looking back at Gary, and he takes his hand back from my leg to pound it on the wheel. I hold my breath as he stops short, does a three-point turn, and goes back to the turn. "Just kidding!" he yells.

I close my eyes, thinking of Liz and Ashley in the back-seat. They don't know I flirted, enticing him. If something happens, it will be my fault. Three girls in a strange man's car. Three girls killed.

"It'll be OK," I hear Liz whisper, always the older sister.

At the next turn he does it again. We're only a few miles from my house now, yet it seems a hundred miles away.

Finally, at the end of my street, he stops the car. "Hmm," he says to Gary. "Maybe I won't take them home after all." Gary laughs nervously.

"Come on," I say. "That's not funny."

That's when Tim notices me again, and he puts his hand back on my thigh. I can hear Ashley crying softly behind me. His hand inches beneath my skirt, toward my crotch.

"OK, OK," he says. "I guess I'll take you all the way." He grins. "Get it, Gary? I'll take them *all the way*."

I squirm, but it's no use. His coarse fingers worm up to my underwear, scratching and grabbing as I try to pull away. They're my best underwear, lavender in color, and he traces the edges with his fingertips. I put them on that eve-ning with the thought that just maybe I would get to third base with one of the boys from the city. It seems a long time ago that we were in my house, full of expectation, getting ready for the night. Now he holds his fingers against my crotch – not inside, just against – letting me know he is there. I clench my body, my eyes turned to the window. I want to scream, to push his hand away, but I'm too afraid. Too afraid if I don't give in, he won't let me go at all. But there's something else, too, something growing inside me, something I don't really want to admit: There's another part that's not afraid at all. I almost like it. I know what's happening isn't right. But his touch is an inevitable result of the evening. It is my greatest hope – to be wanted. And here, with this repulsive older man, I am getting that. He holds his hand there like he owns me, but really, silently, I'm the one who owns him.

Tim drives slowly, his hand up my skirt, along my street. Where before I gave directions, I don't now. I don't want him knowing which house is mine. When he is within a few hundred feet, I say hoarsely, "This is fine."

"Yeah?" He turns to me, an intimate, almost friendly look on his face, a look that suggests we are sharing something special. I keep my own face even.

"Stop the car," I say. Tim smiles, a menacing smile, but he does. I throw open the door and pull away from him, and I hear Liz and Ashley open the door in back. His hand slips away, and I feel the slow release of my muscles, the relief, like air squeaking out from an almost bursting balloon. The sky is lightening. Birds sing a crazed chorus from the trees. Ashley, Liz, and I run up my driveway, looking back a few times to make sure the car leaves, which it does. My mother is asleep, unaware, so we sneak in, using this as our excuse to not speak about what happened. I pull out cots and sleeping bags, and the three of us lie with our eyes closed, our bodies exhausted, but unable to sleep. I cup my hand over my crotch, aware of the ghost of pressure I still feel there. When my mother wakes, I figure, I'll come up with some story: Ashley's mother drove us here early so she can clean their house, and now we're tired because we've been up all night telling ghost stories. Some story suggesting we're still young, untouched, still safe from our own desires and from the world of men.

◆ ◆ ◆

AS SUMMER TURNS to fall, my mother makes a decision. She wants to go to medical school. She's been working as an artist, making jewelry, sculpture, and paintings. But her father was a doctor, and an artist's hands can morph easily into a surgeon's. Besides, she needs to find a way to make a living now. She's used to a particular way of life – a doctor's daughter, and then an engineer's wife. Art isn't going to cut it.

This all feels strange, even unlikely, as if my mother has suddenly become someone else. She was always an artist, always eccentric and avant-garde, not a serious doctor in a white coat. My mother's friends were all unconventional too. They lived in lofts in SoHo and made large, crazy paintings right there in their living rooms. They put on performances in which Tyler and I got to wear red, purple, and blue sheer scarves and prance across the stage. They were often gay and silly – or just plain silly – and I loved them. When my parents were still together they hosted summertime parties, and our house was filled with all those silly, laughing adults. The Rolling Stones and Fleetwood Mac boomed from the speakers my father had moved outside, and Tyler and I twirled around in the warm darkness, dancing and laughing, allowed to stay up late.

Because of this, because of how different her life will be as a doctor, I ask her if she's sure.

"I've *always* wanted to be a doctor," she tells Tyler and me, as though this were something obvious we had missed.

"You'll make a great doctor." Tyler hugs her, always supportive, but I know she feels it too. I can tell by the fear I see, hidden like a squirmy puppy she's not supposed to have brought home.

So Mom starts a year-long pre-med program at the local college and prepares for her application to medical school. She piles the desk in her bedroom with fat textbooks. She fills pages of notebook paper with her neat drawings of cells and neurons. She closes the door and tells us we have to be quiet so she can study. And she invites an Australian college exchange student to stay in the guest room to help pay the mortgage.

Antony is extremely handsome, with light brown hair, dark eyebrows, and bright blue eyes. Liz makes a point of spending the night more often, and the two of us follow Antony around, teasing and flirting. He's twenty-one years old, but he tolerates our behavior. He calls us cute, which we discuss later. Can cute mean sexy? My mother often says I'm cute, and I assumed that meant I looked like a baby. But now I'm not so sure. I examine my features, my freckled nose, big eyes like Mom's. Maybe cute is one step away from something better, just an angling of the hips or the way I hold my head. I practice different looks in the mirror, seeing what's possible.

Tyler stays away from all of us, bothered by the changes, but I see Antony as an opportunity. This is my chance to learn about men. I do everything I can to entice him. I take a long time walking from my bath back to my room, a towel wrapped around my pubescent body, hoping Antony will catch a glimpse. I wear shirts that hug my small breasts and old nightgowns so thin you can see the outline of my figure. At night, I fantasize he will come to my room, unable to control himself any longer, drawn in by my magnetism, and make love to me. I want to experience that kind of attention. My mother flirts with him too, laughing and flashing him smiles. One night she pours them both glasses of wine and invites him to sit with her on the screened-in porch. I hear them chatting, his voice measured, hers too loud and peppered with giggles. A couple of hours later he goes back to his room and closes the door. I know my mother must be lonely, suddenly without the husband she had for fifteen years. Having someone around must be familiar, comfortable, like the way my father touches his girlfriend now. Sometimes I can see why my mother is so hurt. She was on the other side of those touches once. My father knew her in such an intimate way. But her flirting with Antony seems pathetic, desperate. I'm embarrassed by her need. Worse, I fear my need isn't all that different. Antony is no more interested in a twelve-year-old girl than he is in a woman in her forties. Like my mother, I want to be known by someone too. But it doesn't happen for either of us, and after a couple of months, Antony moves out when his student visa expires.

◆ ◆ ◆

ONE MORNING, NOT long after Antony has gone, Tyler asks our mother what it feels like to be kissed. We're getting ready to leave the house for school. Our ride is a teacher who takes all the kids from New Jersey to the school in Riverdale, and he is already waiting at the end of the driveway. I busy myself with the buttons on my coat, not wanting either of them to see that I know the answer to Tyler's question. My mother smiles.

"It's a nice feeling," she says as she wipes a counter. "Soft."

Tyler wraps a scarf around her neck, listening.

"I can show you." My mother steps toward Tyler, the sponge still in her hand, and she leans down and kisses her on the mouth. Tyler nods.

"Oh," she says.

I move toward the door, wanting to get away.

"Kerry?" Mom asks. "Do you want to feel it too?"

I shake my head quickly, avoiding her stare. "Come on," I tell Tyler. "We're late."

"Relax, Kerry," Mom says, a note of anger in her voice. "Always in such a hurry. You need to learn to relax."

Another day, I hear my mother and sister in the kitchen. As I approach I slow down to listen.

"You're growing so much," Mom says, water running as she washes dishes. "Becoming a woman. You have breasts now."

"I know, Mom, but—" Tyler protests.

"They have lots of sensations," Mom goes on. "Did you know that? It can feel nice to have someone touch them."

This is when I reach the doorway. My sister sits at the counter, her eyes on the TV. My mother steps up behind her and puts her hands on my sister's breasts. I am briefly aware I could do something. I could storm in and question my mother. I could call Tyler's name. But then my mother lets her hands fall at her sides, and goes back to the sink. It is just a moment, so quick it could have not happened at all. My sister stares at the television, her body still. My mother at the sink. I step back, away from them, having done nothing.

My mother takes her MCAT, sends in her medical school applications, and gets rejected one by one. She calls her father, who speaks with one of his former students, now running the international pre-med program in the Philippines, and it is set. She will leave in a few months. One evening, I sit at the kitchen counter, doing home-work. I can hear my mother and sister talking in another part of the house, sharing something private, as they often do. Their voices rise and fall. And suddenly, they are in the kitchen with me, a whirlwind of movement and energy. Tyler holds something, crying. Mom tries to wrench it from her hand. Tyler grabs a glass and fills it with water from the kitchen tap.

"I don't want to live," Tyler screams between sobs. I see then the bottle in her hand. Tylenol. She opens the top, pushing Mom's hand away, and pours the bottle into her mouth.

"No!" Mom screams. She digs her fingers into Tyler's mouth, pulling out the pills and flinging them away. Tyler clenches her mouth, but finally she releases against my mother, both of them sobbing and holding on to each other.

I sit still at the counter, my hands gripped tightly together in my lap. My mother and my sister stay like this, unaware of me perhaps, or else unconcerned. So intimate I finally have to look away.

My grandparents fly into town to stay with us the month Mom plans to leave. They help Mom pack, and my grandmother makes dinners so Mom doesn't have to. They take Tyler and me to play miniature golf, giving Mom some space, and Grandpa takes me on long walks like when I visited them in Florida, like we did when life was simple and containable – a firefly caught in a jar.

Grandma reminds us often what a strong, brave thing our mother is doing, going off into the world to pursue her dream to become a doctor. She needs our support. She holds a tone in her voice when she says this, a tone warning us not to make Mom feel bad. The day my mother is to leave for Manila, my grandparents drive us all to the airport. My mother cries loudly at the gate, clutching onto Tyler who, heeding our grandmother's warning, tells her everything will be OK. Tyler's face is flat, without expression. She looks small and empty to me, a deflated doll. When my mother turns her wet eyes to me, I just shrug. I refuse to give her what she wants. She made her choice. Let her sit in it. Why should I care about her sadness now? Besides, in many ways her leaving is a relief. No more of her constant need for attention. No more ducking her all-consuming emotions. I give her a quick hug, trying not to inhale her familiar scent. Deep inside, though, her leaving takes its grip. A fishhook latching into my bones. Years later, when I am in college and driving back to my apart-ment, I will hear a psychologist on the radio discussing divorce, talking about how the scariest part of divorce for children is their fear that if one parent left, perhaps the other one will leave too. I will pull over, the pain rising into my throat, fresh and raw as that day in the airport.

My grandparents help my mother make her way down the tarmac with her bags. Tyler and I stand, silent, and watch her go. A month later, we move in with our dad.

Two

BEFORE BOYS PUT their soft, eager hands on my skin, before they pull me into dark rooms and whisper promises I hold on to like rope pulling me from water, before I sink further and further into trouble, I have crushes. Most girls know what it's like to long for boys in this way, to see the smooth, olive-toned skin of some boy and have their hearts start racing. Overwhelmed by both my mother's needs and her absence, that sensation feels like desperation.

Boys are unknown to me. When my father moved out, women surrounded me. My mother's anxious insecurity, her long talks with girlfriends at the kitchen counter, my sister's sadness, these are the things that made up my life. The times my sister and I visited my father in his one-bedroom apartment were always a relief. There was room to breathe. There was no talk about emotions. Even now, at thirteen, living with him without my mother there to temper it, he seems distant and airy, more like a friend than a parent. It is all computer games and Doritos and music turned up loud.

Boys are connected to this independence for me. I've seen the movies, read the books. I know the ways a boy can make a girl feel. I believe they have the capacity to pull me out of the muck of my life, to save me, and I will believe this for a long, long time.

Once ninth grade starts, Liz and I spend time in Leonia, a nearby town, to hang out with her boyfriend, Chris. Her grandmother lives there, and we arrive each Friday after school with our packed duffels. Liz calls Chris, and soon we are walking to the playground behind the library to meet him and his friends. Brian is one of these friends – a dark-haired, quiet, hard boy who is rarely around. When he is, he barely seems to notice me. Liz told me Brian once liked her, and even though Liz has an insecure way of puffing herself up, I believe her. Why wouldn't he like her? She is beautiful, skinny, and fun to be around. I, on the other hand, am mousy. My thighs touch (a no-no, according to *Seventeen* magazine), childish freckles cover my nose, and my hair never does what I want it to. It makes perfect sense that he ignores me. But that doesn't stop my desire for him. It eggs it on. He is unreachable, a fantasy, like all those movie boys. Plus, he is bad.

One afternoon I watch him come from the library, a book in his hand. Chris, Liz, a few other kids, and I hang out on the play structure at the playground. I sit dangling my legs off the top of the slide. As Brian crosses the playground, he tears something from the book and lets it float behind him to the ground. Then he walks on. As soon as he is out of view I slide down and get what he dropped. It's a library pocket for a checkout ticket. He stole a book about Jimi Hendrix. I stuff it into the back pocket of my tight jeans. Chris, who had watched all this, puts an arm around my shoulder.

"Sorry," he says and smiles. Chris is great-looking as well, with full lips and big eyes. I smile back, embarrassed at having been seen. In some ways, I harbor a crush on Chris, too. But he's Liz's and therefore off-limits.

The three of us and a guy everyone calls Dino walk down the Leonia streets toward Chris's house, looking for something to do. I hope Brian will show up again, but know it's unlikely. It is October and darkness is coming early. Most of the trees are already straggly and bare. Chris and Liz hold hands, and Chris tells us about an ex-girlfriend who used to call him every hour just to know where he was. We all laugh at how crazy this girl was. Newly fourteen, I know girls shouldn't be so demanding. It is one of the many rules I am slowly learning, rules for what boys like and don't like. I store them in my mind, knowing I need to keep them close if I ever want a boy to like me back.

Chris's parents aren't home, so we settle into his living

room and turn on the TV. After a while Chris and Liz disappear. It's no secret they've gone off to mess around. The envy I feel is a low ache in my pelvis. I want a boyfriend like Chris. I sit on the worn, yellow couch, and Dino sits across from me in a La-Z-Boy. Chris's house is small. It's clear from the décor his family doesn't have much money. Most people in Leonia don't. My mother sent Tyler and me to private school, believing her children should have only the best. But I know only rich people can make such choices. I also know my mother doesn't like that she can't control where we go and who we spend time with anymore, now that she's gone. She would be unhappy if she knew I was spending time with someone like Dino, and this pleases me to no end.

Dino doesn't say anything. He pulls out a joint and lights it. He takes a long drag, then holds it out to me. I take it, even though I don't really like to smoke pot. I don't like the way it makes me feel full of dread, like I'm forgetting something important, like something dangerous is about to occur. I put it to my mouth quickly, inhaling only a small amount. A cough sits in my throat but I hold it there. I pass back the joint, and Dino sucks on it some more. He is older than the rest of us, maybe eighteen, and he is notorious for his drug use. Chris says if there's nothing else around, Dino buys glue to sniff. He has a shaved head and acne scars on his cheeks, and he always wears the same black leather motorcycle jacket. Looking at him now, I think he could be OK-looking if he wasn't working so hard to be ugly.

Dino and I pass the joint back and forth. Then he moves to sit next to me on the couch. Chris and Liz are still gone, but I don't know how long it's been, the pot curling its way into my sense of time. Dino, wordless, slips an arm around my shoulder, takes a long drag, and then presses his lips on mine. I flinch, but he is strong. He opens his mouth and blows, shooting the smoke into my throat. I cough, pulling away, and Dino laughs. His jacket sleeve shifts as he holds the joint up to his mouth again, and I see small, jagged knife cuts on his forearm. I wonder what it must be like to be him. Surely there's a reason he does all the drugs. I don't really want Dino to touch me. He smells like old smoke and unwashed clothes, and as far as I can tell he hasn't brushed his teeth in a while. But I'm also not about to refuse him. I want him to like me. This matters more than anything else. Maybe those knife marks point to a soft part of him of which I could be a piece. Maybe Dino is just looking to be loved, like me. So I let his tongue in the next time he leans forward. It tastes sharp from the smoke. I close my eyes and try to imagine this is Brian, which helps as Dino slides a hand up my shirt and kneads at my breasts. He unzips my jeans and pushes a rough hand down there, and soon his finger is inside me. I lean back, keeping Brian in my mind, knowing I should enjoy it, but Dino's movements are too forceful. After a moment he takes my hand and pulls it to his jeans. Obedient, I reach inside and feel the warm, clammy shaft of his penis. It's the first penis I've ever touched. I've never even seen a penis before, except for pictures in books, and my cousin's from when we had shown each other our genitals when we were seven. I've never been this close, though, this intimate. It seems wrong, like I'm touching something I shouldn't, something not for me. Still, I stroke it, knowing this is what he wants, and he pushes his fingers farther into me, which hurts. I stay silent, numb even, as I stroke and fondle until he comes onto my hands. He pushes me away, embarrassed it seems, and takes his fingers out of me. I don't look at him. I'm embarrassed too. I quickly stand, zip, and go to find a bathroom to wash the hot, messy liquid off my hand.

When I come back, Dino is in the other chair again, rolling another joint. I sit back on the couch. He barely looks at me, and it occurs to me we've never exchanged more than a few words. I don't even know his real name. I try to think of something to say, something that will relieve the tension I'm feeling.

"I guess Chris and Liz are having a good time," I say.

He keeps his eyes on what he's doing and shrugs.

"What time is it?" I ask next.

Dino just shrugs again. "Fuck if I know."

I bite my lip, feeling stupid. He doesn't want to talk. So

I turn to the TV, some game show, and try not to think too much about what we've just done.

By the time Chris and Liz come into the room, it's late, so we go back toward the playground. Dino finds a stick on the ground and whacks at tree branches as we walk, trying to knock them down. Every once in a while he exclaims as the stick hits: "Gotcha! Bam!"

Liz tells me she and Chris sixty-nined. She's proud. Sixty-nining is a new trend, an achievement of sorts, making its way through our school. I don't tell her what I did with Dino. It's not that I regret it. That's not quite it. I'm just embarrassed. Nobody fools around with Dino. He's the town druggie, the one we laugh about when he isn't there. And then there's the fact that he hasn't said a word to me since. My crotch is sore from his fingers, and though it hurts I kind of like it. I like the proof someone's been there. Someone wanted me enough to touch me. I watch him jump to reach a branch and break it off, and I wonder what he thinks about what happened. If he is thinking about it at all.

◆ ◆ ◆

A COUPLE OF months later, I have a party. My father is out of town for business, as he commonly is, leaving my sister and me alone. He thinks things will be fine. Tyler has grown withdrawn and silent since my mother left, and he knows nothing about how I spend my time. He defines his approach to parenting as, "If your grades are fine and you look basically OK, then I don't need to know." My mother, I am sure, would be appalled. Tyler's and my bedrooms are at the end of a hallway, and I see my dad many times rush past the hallway without turning his head. He speaks freely about it, as though he has formulated a confident parenting style, but I think both Tyler and I know he's simply afraid of us. He grew up with two brothers, and we're teenage girls. As much as I feel boys are foreign to me, he must feel the same about girls.

The evening of the party I pray Brian will show up. Chris promised me he told him about it. My father is renovating our kitchen, and there are appliances in boxes – a microwave, a new coffee maker. Tiles are stacked out on the veranda. Liz, Chris, and I pass around a forty of Budweiser as we wait for people to arrive, and I start to get a little buzzed. Dino shows up early, always eager to get to where the beer and drugs might be. He opens a beer and starts collecting money to get some more.

"You want to go in on this?" he asks me. I nod and go to get some money from my purse. I've seen him only twice since the evening we got together, and he has treated me exactly the same as always, with no acknowledgment of what we shared. Mostly, this is a relief. I don't want any repercussions from that night. But a part of me wants something, anything. A wink, a hand squeeze, something. After all, I've never been so intimate with a boy before.

When I come back, money in hand, my heart leaps into my throat. Brian stands talking with Dino, his dark hair hanging into his eyes. He's here, in my home, talking to the guy I was close with. In my crushed-out mind, it's almost as though we've been close too. I hand Dino my money.

"Hey," I say to Brian.

"Hey," he says back.

My body tingles.

"We're going to take off to get the beer," Dino says. "Want to come?"

It's my party, my home, and people are starting to arrive in droves. But I don't hesitate. This is my chance to be with Brian. "Sure," I say.

We take the elevator to the lobby and walk to Dino's car, an old Buick. Brian holds the seat forward as I climb in back, hoping he's checking out my butt. Then he gets in and messes with Dino's stereo. The car smells predictably like stale smoke and decaying upholstery. I watch Brian from the backseat, desperate for him to notice me.

"I'm so stupid to leave my own party," I blurt.

Brian doesn't say anything, and I immediately regret having spoken. I think of the rules. Boys like girls who are quiet, mysterious, who suggest but don't blurt. I know this, but it's still so hard for me. The desperation I feel is always too there, too much. I don't know how to quiet it, a yappy dog that just won't shut up.

At the convenience store, Dino jumps out, the motor still running, leaving Brian and me alone. Brian turns up the radio as a Jimi Hendrix song starts.

"I love this song," I say. Brian glances back at me, and I close my eyes and move my shoulders suggestively to the music.

"You like Jimi Hendrix?" he asks.

"Love him," I say, which is only sort of true. "I can put him on when we get back to my place."

"Cool." Brian nods. My head is light, full of excitement. I'm making a connection with Brian.

When we arrive at my apartment, it is full with people I mostly don't know, many of them way too old to be at a fourteen-year-old-girl's party. But I don't care. Brian was talking to me. I go straight to the stereo, which someone else has commandeered, find my father's Hendrix album, and put it on the turntable.

The guy who was working the stereo looks down at me, pissed.

"This is my apartment," I say. He backs off. Once the music starts, I beeline back to Brian. Liz, looking worried, stops me.

"Do you know any of these people?" she asks.

"I'll deal with it later," I say.

"But, Kerry, they're in your dad's room. They're all over. Chris and I can't control them."

"I'll figure something out," I say. Anxiety shoots

through me. I know Liz is right. I know I need to take control of the situation.

But … Brian.

This is my chance with Brian.

I continue toward him. He opens a beer, takes a long sip, and I watch his Adam's apple move. I follow his lead, open a beer myself, and down a few sips. Just enough to make me fearless. "Come with me," I say to him.

I grab his arm and pull him through the crowd of people into my father's room. There are five people in there, none of whom I recognize. One has a mustache and he's rifling through my father's drawer.

"Hey," I say. "What are you doing?" The guy looks up and shuts the drawer. He shrugs and he and the others amble out. "Nobody's allowed in here," I say as I shut the door behind them, trying not to think about the fact that my father keeps personal things in his drawers, things like drugs and, I was pretty sure, a gun.

I turn to look back at Brian. Brian, Brian. I am in here alone with Brian.

He looks at me, his expression mild. I move quickly, before I lose my nerve, and I push him toward my father's bed. He raises his eyebrows with surprise, but before he can say or do anything I press my lips to his. I force him onto the bed, one leg on either side of his hips. I lose myself, letting myself be a girl I assume boys want, sexual and willing, a girl who will sixty-nine.

"Hey," he says.

I say nothing, just push at his shirt, tug at his pants. I kiss his chest and neck, ravenous as a wild dog. I need to get in there, to show him I'm desirable. I think of Dino and how he led my hand there. I don't know a lot about boys, but it's common knowledge they're slaves to their penises. I want to show Brian what I know, teach him to want me through my hands. I am vaguely aware of the muffled noises of the party on the other side of the door. Music reverberates through the wall. I allow it to guide me, give me a rhythm as I work my way down his body. But Brian pushes me off.

"Jesus," he says. He straightens his shirt, checks his pants. He gives me a look, a look like I've gone over the edge, like I'm a crazy girl, like the one Chris talked about that night, one of the girls the boys stayed away from. I look back, chest tight, ashamed, horrified, wanting to say something. Something that will tell him he misunderstood. I'm not crazy. I just like him. Maybe a little too much. But he turns away and walks out of the room.

Liz comes running to find me right after. Some guys are stealing boxes out of the kitchen. She says she and Chris are getting everyone out; the party needs to end. Soon the only people left are Chris, Liz, and me. Even Dino has gone home, hearing a rumor of cops on their way. I didn't see Brian leave.

I look around the apartment. Beer cans and bottles are strewn around the floor and countertops, on top of the stereo and TV. A few have toppled, leaking beer into the carpet. I see two cigarette burns in the couch. I walk down the hallway to my room to find it ransacked, as is Tyler's. Cigarette butts and cans are on every conceivable surface. The corner of Tyler's Siouxsie and the Banshees poster is ripped. Apparently someone threw around her collection of fantasy books and figurines, and now they lay scattered about the room. I'm relieved to find none of them damaged. As Liz and I step through the mess, though, we find a used condom near Tyler's bed.

In the living room, one of the speakers has a long rip down the middle. Tiles are littered and broken on the terrace. The pile of new appliances is all but gone. And, when I look in my dad's drawer, the drugs are gone and there's no gun. I wish so much that I could remember if there was one in there before.

We move through the rooms, filling trash bags and hauling them out to the garbage chute. Nobody says much. We work with calm diligence, sharp counterpoint to the panic inside. Liz vacuums and I wipe the counter-tops with Lysol, but the apartment still smells like someone poured beer over everything.

Tyler comes home first, after staying at a friend's for the night.

"Nobody better have touched my stuff," she tells me. She's wearing black, as usual. Big, loose clothes that hide her body.

"No one wanted to go into your stupid room," I say. I don't dare tell her about the condom.

When she comes out later, she says, "You owe me a poster."

My dad arrives home soon after, and I'm in a lot of trouble. He's facing two $3,000 lawsuits, one from the building because someone thought it would be fun to throw tiles off the deck, ripping the pool cover, and another from a person whose parked car was hit by tiles as well. Dad says nothing to me about the possibly missing gun or the drugs, but I'm sure he's pretty fumed about that as well.

He decides to move me to another private school and forbid me from seeing Liz. Liz and I say a tearful good-bye on the phone. We sob about how unfair life is, and how when we can, when all of this is in the past, we'll find each other again. After I hang up, I lie back on my bed and look out the window, from which I can see the Manhattan skyline. My life is about to change yet again. I close my eyes, seeing how this feels, and I realize I don't really mind. Change doesn't scare me. I know about change. I may even like it. I'll have a fresh start with new classmates and friends. Particularly, I'll meet new boys. Boys who might see me as something more than just a friend. I definitely don't want to see Brian or Dino again. I exposed myself. This is my chance to renew who I am, try again to be the self-controlled, mysterious girl, the one who lives by the rules. It's my first of many attempts to start from scratch in this way, to try again and again to swallow my desperation, claw my way up from under it.

Three

GYM IS THE most embarrassing of high school classes. We have to change in the locker room in front of one another, everything revealed – heavy breasts, thick hips, and unshaved legs. This is especially bad for the new girl. I am sharply aware of the moles on my arms, the way my leg fat spreads if I sit to pull on jeans. The other girls, already in cliques, chatter away, every once in a while stealing glances my way. I push the dirty gym clothes into the locker and duck out, avoiding eyes. It is in this vulnerable state, making my way back toward the other buildings, that Amy stops me.

"Did you just start here?" she asks. She looks at me with sharp brown eyes. She is bigger than me, both in stature and in height, and I feel vaguely intimidated. I recognize her from campus. She's a grade ahead of me.

I nod.

"Why?" she asks.

"Why?" I'm confused.

"Why are you coming here for tenth grade?" She keeps her gaze steady. "Did you just move?"

"I got in trouble," I tell her. "My dad made me switch schools."

Amy's eyes open wide, intrigued. "What did you do?"

I shrug. "I had a party and people stole stuff." Amy smiles slightly and seeing her amusement, I keep going, embellishing. "And there were boys. I did some things my dad didn't like."

Now Amy's smile fills her face. "I know what that's like," she says.

I smile too.

From then on, Amy and I spend most of our time together. On weekends we take cabs into Manhattan and search for bars that won't badger us for our fake IDs. Our aim is simple: We're looking for boys.

Most nights, Dad sleeps at his new girlfriend's, leaving Amy and me free to do what we want. Amy calls her mother, telling her she'll be sleeping over. I can tell from Amy's brief silence that her mother begins to protest, but Amy always cuts her off.

"I'll be fine, Sheila," she says, annoyed, and she rolls her eyes at me. I shake my head, feigning understanding, but the truth is I am amazed by the way she talks to her mother. She even calls her by her first name! I would never have the guts.

Nights that Dad is home, he watches me carefully as I emerge with Amy from the hallway, both of us wearing miniskirts and too much makeup. He knows he shouldn't trust us. But I can tell he also kind of likes it, even after that whole lawsuit thing last year. He likes that I try to be pretty, that I'm even becoming pretty as I get older, and he likes that I want to party. It reminds him of who he used to be when he was a teen, when he was popular and carefree, not a divorced dad raising two girls by himself. He has stories, like the one from when he was seventeen and working at Jan's Ice Cream Parlor with his friend Les. Whenever thirteen- or fourteen-year-old girls visited, they told the girls to sit tight while they prepared a special treat: two scoops of vanilla ice cream, a carefully carved banana, whipped cream, and chocolate sprinkles for pubic hair.

"Here you go," my young father said. "Virgin's Delight, made especially for you."

The girls erupted into giggles. They held their spoons this way and that, trying to work at the ice cream.

My father and Les winked at them. "What's the matter? Don't you like it? Is it too big for you?"

They giggled some more.

I can tell by the way he talks that he misses those days.

Tyler is another story. Tyler stays in her room with the door closed. I think it bothers Dad that he doesn't understand her the way he does me. She's too much like Mom, with her interest in art and all things alternative. She even looks like her, dark-haired and small. I avoid looking at her door as I pass, not wanting to think about the way she isolates herself all the time. It's her choice, I tell myself. She could be going out and having fun if she wanted to. No one's making her sit around with her fantasy figurines, waiting for Mom to call.

"Where are you going?" Dad asks when I head for the front door. His cigarette sits in an ashtray on the coffee table, swirling smoke into the air.

"To the city," I say. "I told you."

"I want you home by midnight."

"Dad." I cross my arms. "Nothing even happens until ten."

Dad takes a deep breath, considering this. "How about one?"

I scowl.

"Two?"

"Fine." I glance over at Amy, roll my eyes. And we leave.

"I wish my dad were like that," Amy says once we're in the elevator. I think of her dad, who owns a chicken-packing company. He leaves every day at four in the morning, so usually when I'm at Amy's house he's asleep. When he's awake, he's grouchy and distant. He calls Amy "Lame-y" as a joke, but I can tell Amy doesn't think it's funny. In many ways I do feel lucky my dad is my dad. He's friendly and funny – really funny, not mean funny – and he smokes pot in the apartment. My friends have always liked him, and I can tell he takes pride in being the cool dad.

We find the taxi we ordered idling outside my building and get in. Both of us have piles of twenties in our purses, courtesy of our dads. The ride into Manhattan is always the same for me. As we cross the bridge I can see the endless lights that make up the skyline, flickering like a secret code. The sky is pale, starless, no match for the life below. The excitement of the city enters my bones like drugs from a syringe, and by the time we are paying and getting out on the Upper West Side, I am convinced something real can happen, something that can change my life. We walk to the West End, a trendy bar full of underagers like ourselves. The sweaty, bearded bouncer smirks at our IDs, but he leans back to let us through. Amy goes to the bar and orders us sea breezes. Not that it matters to anyone working there, but we don't really care about the drinks. We're not looking to get drunk. We just order them to have something to do with our hands in case there are no tables. It's the same reason we light up cigarettes. We take our drinks and look around the room. Sure enough, the tables are full, so we stand against the wall, bouncing our heads just slightly to the music blaring from the ceiling. The bar is loud tonight, full of laughter and conversation. Amy and I look at each other, trying to think of something to talk about. This too, looking like we're engaged in intense conversation, is a part of looking right, like we're not really just waiting for some boys to approach us and free us from our discomfort.

These minutes, the waiting, this is always the worst for me. My anxiety peaks, wondering whether I will be picked, like waiting to be chosen for a team in gym class. I run my fingers through my hair, cross one leg in front of the other, hoping that makes me look thinner. I scan the room, doing my best to look available, but not wanting to betray the desperation inside. I talk casually with Amy, but inside I am a jumble of angst and prayers. *Please*, I think, *please let a boy find me tonight.*

This particular night, I see Amy has noticed someone.

"Look," she says, pointing her chin toward someone. Then, as I turn to look, "No, not so obvious." I stop myself and glance back as casually as I can. There are three boys there, two OK-looking and one very good-looking. I recognize them immediately. It's Peter R and his friends from our school, seniors. Every girl wants to date Peter. An extremely pretty senior girl did for a few months, but it was over quickly, and as far as I know no one has dated him since.

"I didn't know anyone from school came here," I say.

"Me neither." She grabs my arm. "Come on."

We make our way toward them, my heart thumping against my chest. They look up with amused expressions.

"Hello, ladies," one of Peter's friends says. "Can we be of service?"

Peter and the other one chuckle and exchange looks. I swallow, hoping they aren't making fun.

"We know you," Amy says to Peter. "We go to Dwight too."

Peter raises his eyebrows and smiles.

"Really?" He stands. "I'll get you some chairs."

I breathe out, relieved, and we smile at the other two, Danny and Case. Peter comes back with chairs, and we set our drinks on the table and sit.

"So, what grade are you guys in?" Case asks. He has light brown hair and a long nose.

We tell them.

"I recognize you," Danny says to me. "You're new this year."

I nod, feeling good. He knows about me. I'm noticeable. I take a long sip of my drink and light up a cigarette. As I blow out I look right at Peter.

"How long have you guys been here?" I ask.

Peter looks back at me. His eyes are a pale blue, and his blond hair hangs over them. He lights up a cigarette too. I put a finger to my lips, wanting him to think about them, to imagine kissing me. "I don't know," he says. "A few hours."

"Let's do something," I say. I look at Amy and she smiles.

"We could go to the park," she says, referring to Central Park.

"Nah." Danny downs the rest of his beer. His dark curls are cut close to his head, but he runs a hand over them as though they are long. "We can go to my place."

I look at Peter. He shrugs and finishes his beer too. My heart picks up pace again as the five of us leave the bar and walk to Danny's car, a white Honda. He opens the back door and Amy and I climb in. To my delight, Peter climbs in after me. I lift my leg slightly, so it will look thinner, and then I press it, just barely, against Peter's. He glances at me, but I keep my eyes straight ahead. I don't want to overwhelm him. I want him to come to me.

We drive through the city streets and head over the bridge, Led Zeppelin's "Immigrant Song" blaring from the radio. The boys laugh at private jokes, and Amy and I smile at each other. We're getting what we wanted. I mouth to her, "Peter is mine."

She raises her eyebrows. "Good luck," she mouths back.

Danny turns off an exit and down some side roads and we slow in front of a moderate-sized house. We follow him inside and go straight to his bedroom.

"Where are your parents?" Amy asks.

"Asleep." Danny throws a bunch of clothes off his unmade bed. "Just don't get too loud."

Case laughs, hearing the sexual innuendo. I laugh too, looking right at Peter.

Peter sits on a beanbag chair on the floor, and I sit against the wall beside him, trying to figure out how to get him alone. Danny puts a Doors album on, and when he leaves the room to find beer in the kitchen, I get an idea.

"I need a cigarette," I say softly, just to Peter. "Come with me?"

"Where?" I can't read his expression. Is he hesitating? Does he not want to be alone with me?

"Is there a deck? Or on the front stoop. I don't know." I stand up, close to him, so he can feel the heat from my legs. I see him glance at them briefly.

"I guess I could go for a cigarette," he says, and I know I have him. He stands and as we walk out of the room, I smile slyly at Amy.

Look at me, I'm thinking. *Getting Peter R alone.*

I follow Peter to sliding doors that lead to a deck. Danny sees us on his way back to his bedroom but says nothing. This gives me some hope. Maybe he expected Peter to want to be intimate with me, away from the others. It is a chilly spring night. I hold my jean jacket closed. I pull out a cigarette, hand one to Peter, and he lights them. The night is clear, a half moon glowing in a corner of the sky. Stars sprinkle above the dark trees in Danny's backyard. That discomfort kicks in again, the wondering and waiting. I take a drag and try to think of something to say, something that will cut into my anxiety.

"Tenth grade, huh," Peter says. I smile, relieved he spoke first.

"Is there a problem with that?"

He smiles too. "I don't really spend time with sophomores."

"You're too good for us."

He shrugs. "I didn't say that."

I watch his lips as he talks, wishing he would just kiss me already. I don't want to have this conversation that pulls me just barely from my anxiety. I want to feel him hovering above me, blocking out all else. I want his full and total attention, and I want it to reach every part of me. Nothing left alone. Nothing untouched. I step toward him and touch his arm.

"What are you saying then?" I ask. I bite my lip.

He lets out a low laugh, understanding what I'm doing. With his eyes on mine he reaches a hand out and touches my breast. It is almost a competitive gesture, a dare. Like he's checking to see what I can handle. I hold my gaze on his. Then I lean forward and kiss him. He kisses me too but then pulls back abruptly. I throw my cigarette over the side of the deck, bothered, those nervous questions rushing in again. *Is he teasing? Does he not like me?* He takes another drag and leans his hands against the deck railing.

"Nice night," he says.

I twist my lips in frustration and cross my arms over my front. After a moment, he flicks his cigarette off the side. He lifts the hair off the back of my neck and kisses me there. My whole body tingles, and I stay perfectly still, not wanting him to stop. His kisses are so tender, I could almost cry. He turns me around and kisses me again, this time harder. He bites at the side of my neck, the tenderness gone. Then he pushes me against the deck, grinding himself against me. I can feel him, hard against my belly, and I push back, all body, all pressing and pulling, my thoughts finally gone. He reaches under my shirt. And then all of a sudden he stops again. He pulls back, leaving me breathless, speechless. I reach for him, but he is already walking away, toward the sliding doors. As he slips them open he looks back at me.

"You coming?"

I straighten my shirt and skirt, run a hand through my hair. What just happened? He walks ahead of me, a stranger again. Another boy who doesn't want me. My stomach is hollow, and I realize I am very tired. We go into Danny's room where the three of them are sitting with beer bottles. They look up at us. Danny smiles at Peter, but I don't know what Peter looks like as he grabs a beer from the top of Danny's bureau. I think back to the look Danny gave when he saw us going outside. Maybe he didn't expect Peter to want me. Maybe instead he expected Peter to mess with me like he just did. I hate the elusiveness, not knowing what's going on in their minds. Boys are mysteries with no recognizable clues. They're like aliens, sent to earth with the sole mission of making girls feel like crap. I take a beer too, though I have no desire to drink anymore. I feel deflated and confused. I really just want to go home.

For the next hour, Peter ignores me. I try to stay in the

conversation, but I am too distracted by my thoughts, going over what happened again and again, hoping to figure out what I did wrong. *Did he think I was fat? Was I too eager?* Finally, Amy and I call a cab to go back to my apartment. On the ride home she looks at me.

"Well?" she asks. "Did you get together?"

"Sort of." I keep my gaze out the window, not wanting her to see my expression.

"You either did or you didn't."

I still don't look at her. Even though Amy is interested in boys, it's different with her. She wouldn't let someone play games with her like Peter did with me. She would walk away, lose interest. It's not that she's prettier than me, or even thinner. It's not that I feel inferior to her for these reasons like I used to with Liz. It's the opposite, actually. She struggles with her weight. And I'm prettier than her. I know because when we're at the West End, boys turn to me first. I would never admit it, but I like it this way, not having to see myself as less all the time. Still, Amy wouldn't stand being treated the way Peter had treated me. Why couldn't I do that? Why couldn't I hold myself back, stop being so needy? Needy, just like my mom. I turn to look at Amy, the emptiness in my stomach spreading, turning to anger.

"Look," I say, "we fooled around a little bit. It's not a big deal."

She shakes her head. "Fine," she says. "Relax. I don't

really care anyway." She turns away. "Peter R's a big slut. It's not like you're going to be his girlfriend now anyway."

"I know," I say, but inside I cringe because, of course, like an idiot, that's exactly what I had been hoping for.

When we get home, I go to the bathroom and see two hickeys Peter left on my neck. I touch them, wishing I could keep them there, proof he had wanted me even for a few minutes. But by the time Monday comes, they are mostly faded. I see him only once that week. He walks right by me with a small group of his friends. He doesn't even say hello.

◆ ◆ ◆

BACK AT THE West End, Amy and I stand against a wall with our drinks and cigarettes. "Take On Me" by a-ha floats down from hidden speakers. I sway a little to the music. A few guys approach us, but they are ugly or too old. We turn away from them, hoping to look involved in conversation. Soon, another boy and his friend come in and stand near us. I glance over. Not bad. Not bad at all. One is tall and dark-haired. He looks just a little bit like the guy who played opposite Molly Ringwald in *Sixteen Candles*. Gorgeous. The other one is shorter and stockier with light hair. I angle my body to catch their attention, especially the tall one's. I laugh loudly at something Amy says, throwing my hair back. When I bring the cigarette to my lips, I look right at him. Our eyes meet, and I see a flicker. I've got him.

That night, we wind up at his place. His name is Paul and he lives in a penthouse apartment on Madison Avenue, not far from the Metropolitan Museum of Art. The apartment itself is like a museum, filled with angled leather furniture, abstracts in primary colors on the wall. The kitchen is pure white – cold, glistening – as though nobody ever goes into it. Only Paul's room, where I jerk him off sometime before the sun comes up, has some air of comfort to it.

When Amy and I leave, I write my number on a scratch pad and press it into his hand.

"You'll call?" I ask hesitantly.

"Of course." He laughs and kisses me on the mouth, surprised by my doubt.

Sure enough, Paul does call two evenings later, when I am doing homework and watching television in the living room. We chat briefly and I learn more about him. He's a wrestler at his school, the same school in Riverdale my sister still attends. He's sixteen and his parents let him drive their Porsche sometimes. He invites me to watch him wrestle next Friday, and I hang up smiling. I have a boyfriend. Dad is in the kitchen, and he comes around to where I'm standing.

"Who was that?" he asks, seeing my expression.

"A boy," I say.

He smiles, holding a half-eaten sandwich. This is usually how dinner goes with us. You eat what you can find when you're hungry. "Oh, really." He takes a bite from the sandwich. "What boy is that?"

"He's from Tyler's school. A wrestler."

Dad makes a face that means he's impressed. Is he surprised? I wonder. Does he think I can't get a nice guy? Then his expression changes, but I can't read what he's thinking.

"What?" I say.

"Just don't screw it up."

My stomach sinks. "What's that supposed to mean?"

He smiles. "You know how you can be."

"No," I say, that hollow feeling spreading. "I don't."

"Bossy," he says. "Everything has to be your way."

"Screw you," I say. I walk away from him toward my room. Tears prick my eyes.

"I'm just telling you what boys like," I hear him call after me.

I slam my bedroom door and lie on my bed, hating him, wishing I could be someone else. Not this person who's bossy, who's always aching with need. I get up, pull open a window, and light up a cigarette, a social habit that has quickly become a plain old habit. At the bar cigarettes give me something to do with my hands. Whether by association or because of the chemicals, turns out they calm me elsewhere, too. I hear Tyler rustling around in her room. She's probably closing her own window, annoyed by my smoke wafting in. Not that I have any idea, really, what she's thinking. She never leaves that room, the door is always closed. I've lived with her my whole life, shared childhood baths and well-worn blankets. I've dressed in her hand-me-downs, all scuffed and threadbare from the points and chafes of her body. Her scent is as familiar to me as my own, yet she's a complete stranger to me. I try to put my mind on Paul, reminding myself he's asked me out. Reminding myself someone out there wants to be with me.

Friday Dad drives Amy and me to Riverdale. We step into the gymnasium, where people are scattered in the bleachers. The room smells like sweat and socks. It smells like boys. We take a seat near the front and I spot Paul with his teammates. Like the others, he wears one of those tight halter outfits wrestlers have to wear. They are watching a guy out on the mat who is struggling with a guy from the rival school. Paul's expression is hard. He takes this seriously, that's for sure. The whole scene is sort of silly to me – the outfit, the boys pushing and hugging on the mat, the seriousness. But I push these thoughts away. I want to like Paul. More, I want him to like me. And if becoming interested in wrestling is what I have to do, then so be it.

When it is Paul's turn, he and the other guy thrash about for close to ten minutes, but in the end he pins his opponent. I clap loudly, hoping he'll see me. When the match is over, the bleachers clear out and Amy and I wait, my eyes flicking nervously back to the locker-room doors.

"Does he know you're here?" Amy asks.

I shrug, my anxiety soaring. "He invited me."

"That was back on Monday," she says. She speaks nonchalantly, as though she's not saying something that is making my heart race. "Maybe he forgot."

"He didn't forget," I say quietly.

Then, like an exhaled breath, the door to the locker room opens and a group of boys pushes through. One of them is Paul. He is freshly showered, wearing normal clothes again. He comes right over.

"What did you think?" he asks.

"You were great," I tell him.

"I did OK," he says. "Eight minutes to pinning. But I got him with a neck hold."

I nod, wondering if it means anything that he didn't kiss me hello. "I brought Amy," I say.

"That's cool." He smiles at her. "I'll bring Davis." He calls to one of his friends, a nice-looking boy with curly hair, and we agree to meet in the parking lot where his parents' Porsche is parked.

Back at Paul's apartment, he orders a pizza, and he and Davis eat the whole pie. We sit in the kitchen, and I keep my hands in my lap, afraid to dirty anything. Paul is friendly and kind. He refills my soda. I look up into his dark eyes, wanting him to touch me, to show me he still wants me. Only once does he put a hand on my back briefly as he passes, and the heat where his hand touched stays there the rest of the night until Amy and I leave. He hugs me at the door, a friendly hug, not the sort of hug you give a girlfriend. And I walk away, untouched and cold, like his apartment.

I discuss this with Amy for the next few days.

"Just call him and ask him to do something again," she says. "If he likes you, he'll say yes. If he doesn't, he won't."

She makes it sound so easy, but the possibility of his rejection is unbearable. I don't want more evidence no one will ever like me. At the same time, the wondering is torture. So I call, and, surprising me, he says yes, and we make a plan for the following Saturday. I meet him at his apartment. This time I go alone. We head straight for his bedroom and fool around. My mind slips away, body taking over. *This.* This is what I want. My body in his hands, his face, his breath right there against my skin. It feels good, but not just sexually. His hands, his body, his mouth. He breathes me into being, making me real. I unzip his pants, wanting him to feel what I feel: beholden to me. I want him tied to the memory of me here in his bed. I want him to remember *I* made him feel this good. I kiss down his body as he stretches out, letting me do what I want. At his crotch I stop, thinking about how I can trap him. I had read in a *Cosmopolitan* in my dentist's waiting room about tricks to drive a man wild. One was to challenge him to a sexual game. Every boy loves games.

"I'll bet I can make you come in under two minutes," I whisper, improvising.

"You're on," he says.

So I take his penis into my mouth, and I begin. I have never given a blow job before, so I run through everything I've read or heard about them. Some spot on the head is most sensitive. Some technique they tend to like best. But nothing seems to make a difference. He is not moaning wildly with ecstasy like in the movies. He is not moving at all. My jaw gets tired quickly. Spittle runs out of my mouth. I feel clumsy, amateur. From the corner of my eye I see the red numbers on his clock. The minute changes, and Paul smiles down at me.

"Ha," he says. His voice is controlled. "I win."

I keep going, knowing I have to finish what I started, and after another quick minute or so he comes into my mouth, the hot liquid surprising me. It is gross, but I squeeze my eyes shut and swallow it, suppressing a gag. I heard somewhere guys prefer that. He buttons his pants and gets us water from the kitchen. He remains kind, but a feeling nags at me, staying with me long after I leave. And it's this: It doesn't matter what I did to him. He can choose to remain detached, untouched by me. Something I can't do back.

I call him the next day, and we have a nice conversation. He can't hang out, he says, because he has a lot of home-work, but we can make a plan for the next weekend. In school that week I think of him constantly, twice going silent when called on because I haven't heard the question.

I refer to him as "my boyfriend" when I talk to Amy. I call him three more times, though we only talk once, as he's out the other two. By the time Saturday comes I'm eager to see him, my anxiety high. I need to know he still wants me.

I arrive at his apartment and once again we get right down to business. I give him another blow job, but this time I feel angry while doing it, put out. Afterward, he buttons his pants and goes to the bathroom, leaving me on his bed. When he comes back, I won't look at him.

"What?" he asks.

"You always do that."

"I always do what?" He stands near the door, shock on his face. "What could I possibly *always* do in the time I've known you?"

"Leave me in here."

"I went to the bathroom."

"Whatever," I say. I start putting on my clothes.

"I don't understand what the problem is."

I yank my shirt over my head. A small voice in my head rises up, telling me to stop. I am acting like one of those girls, those needy, crazy girls. But I can't seem to stop it. That feeling – *he doesn't need me, I can't have what I want* – bubbles up, and the words tumble out of my mouth. "The problem is, you don't seem interested in doing anything for me."

He laughs, a short burst. "What are you talking about?"

"Do you even want to be with me?" I ask.

"I've known you for, like, three weeks."

"Forget it," I say. I look down at my bare feet, tears pooling in my eyes.

"Maybe you should go," he says. I look up at him. "The doorman can get you a cab."

I put on my shoes, gather up the rest of my stuff. We say good-bye, and I can tell he is anxious for me to get out of there. I know I've blown it, exposed myself once again. On the ride home, my dad's words echo in my head: *Everything has to be your way.* I look out the window at the lights that line the slopes of the bridge, clutching my purse to my chest.

◆ ◆ ◆

IF MY DAD is home weekend mornings, it means his girlfriend, Nora, is there too. They wake late and spend a long time making breakfast. They cross back and forth in the galley kitchen, opening and closing cupboards, passing knives to chop vegetables for omelets and cream cheese for the bagels. They grind coffee and beat eggs. Sunlight angles in through the silvery blinds, exposing the dust on Dad's granite table that only gets cleaned on Wednesdays when the cleaning lady comes. Usually Nora has a Mets game on the small kitchen TV. Or else it's the Giants. She keeps her eye on the TV and whoops when her team scores. She's the only woman I've ever known who likes sports as much as men. She also has a lot about her that's girly, like the rhinestone clips she wears in her curly hair and the red wire-rimmed glasses she uses for reading. She keeps her nails long and polished, and on these weekend mornings she wears a floor-length, red silky robe she brought from her own apartment in Manhattan. Beneath it I'm pretty sure she's naked. I come into the kitchen and take a fresh carton of orange juice from the refrigerator. Nora stops me.

"Here, honey," she says. "That needs to be shaken."

She takes it from me and starts shaking, putting her whole body into it. Dad comes up behind her and slips a hand around her waist. He makes a noise, a sexual noise, a noise I don't want to hear.

"Put the juice down, babe," he says, "before it reaches climax."

She laughs a little, but she glances at me nervously. I avoid her glance and get a glass down from the cupboard.

"I'll just have water," I say.

I go back to my room where I strip down for a shower. My ritual before a shower is always the same: take off clothes, stand before full-length mirror on the back of my door, curse at my thighs and butt. I have a fantasy I can take scissors and – *snip!* – slice off the flesh I squeeze back from my bones. My mother was constantly dieting when I lived with her, never satisfied with her body. She always looked thin to me, but like her I can't really see what I look like. I rely on what others think, particularly men. From what I understand, men prefer skinny girls, and I believe if I were skinnier I could be lovable.

When I come out of the shower, I hear Tyler talking softly in her room. She opens her door when she hears me, and before she can say so I nod my head. Mom is on the phone. She calls every Sunday, when the rates are down. I put Squeeze on the record player, moisturize, pull on jeans and a sweatshirt, and comb my hair, putting off the inevitable. Finally I lift the receiver in my room. Mom is prattling on about the food she's been eating there – fried bananas and steamed fish.

"Kerry's on the line," Tyler says.

"Hi, sweetie." Mom's voice is clear and loud, as though she is in the next room. "How are you?"

"Fine." I look down at my lap, play with a thread on my sweatshirt.

"How's the new school?"

"Fine," I say again.

"You've made friends?"

I think of Amy, the boys in the bars. "Yes."

Mom sighs and gets quiet. She always gets quiet when she's upset.

"What's the matter, Mom?" Tyler asks softly. Mom takes in a quick breath. "Are you crying?"

"I just wish I could be there with you girls," she sobs.

I close my eyes. *Oh, boy*, I think. *Here we go.*

"We do too," Tyler says.

"It hurts me so much to not be a part of your lives."

"You are a part of our lives," Tyler says. "That hasn't changed."

I look down at my hands to see I am gripping my sweat-shirt. I let go, feeling numb, wishing I didn't have to do this. Wishing I could just hang up the phone, go back to my new life.

"Kerry?" Mom asks. "Are you still there?"

"Yes."

"I hope you know how much I love you."

"OK."

She waits, and finally, just so we can end this already, I tell her what she needs to hear. "I love you, too."

Afterward, when Dad and Nora call us for breakfast, I see Tyler in the hall.

"What?" I say, seeing her look.

"Forget it." She walks off ahead of me, like I'm the one causing her problems. Like feeding Mom what she wants by making her feel better about her choices and then holing up in her room all day is going to make her happy. She has no idea at all.

"What happened to that boy?" Dad asks a few days later. "He never called again?"

"I saw him again," I say, defensive.

Dad puts his hands up, as though to protect himself. "All right, all right," he says. "Don't be so sensitive."

Later, though, knowing I'm upset, he drives me to

Riverside Mall to buy clothes. It's our ritual. His way of doing something for me. It's a cliché, really. The divorced dad buying his daughter's love. He waits on the bench the store provides for dads just like mine, the ones who will tirelessly wait while we, the daughters, try on clothes. And clothes shopping *does* make me feel better, at least briefly, because each new belly-baring top or pair of close-fitting jeans creates one more possibility for me to attract a new boy. And a new boy could mean another chance at love.

Is there another reason girls buy clothes?

At the register, the saleslady tallies the damage: $288 and change. Dad shakes his head and smiles at the woman conspiratorially.

"Daughters," he says. "They're so expensive."

He says the same thing every time.

Four

IT'S LATE SPRING of my sophomore year. Amy turns seventeen and gets a car, and we start going into the city on weekdays as well as weekends. During the week we are able to find open tables. The bars aren't packed. We begin to notice a group of regulars who come in every Tuesday, Wednesday, and Thursday night. This is especially true at a new bar we discover, Dorrian's Red Hand, a dark wood and brass bar on the Upper East Side. The regulars are wealthy high school and college students. The girls are beautiful with slick blond hair and tiny waists. They wear red lipstick and cocktail dresses and have names like Blake and Hunter. The boys are also stunning, many of them wearing navy blue sports jackets with gold insignia from their schools, their ties loosened but still on. Most all of them do cocaine in the bathroom stalls. They pull rolled fifty-dollar bills from their breast pockets and, gripping the brass toilet paper-roll holder for support, they lean over the backs of the toilets where they've assembled the lines.

Amy and I dress accordingly and sit at the same table each night, hoping to fit in, but mostly feeling clunky and unattractive compared to everyone else. Over time, though, a couple of the boys are friendly and sit with us sometimes, and slowly we blend into the culture there. Even though they don't know us, we come to know who most of the regulars are. A tall, handsome boy named Robert, two blond brothers, Chris and Tony. They glide through the bar like movie stars, stopping at tables of girls they know. Robert is gorgeous and charming. The brothers are fun-loving and smooth. Amy and I watch them, enamored.

We are well aware we chose this scene over the others available to us. Some of the kids who mingled at the West End wound up downtown at CBGB's and the Beacon Theater. They don't dress like the regulars at Dorrian's. They wear tight, ripped jeans and Doc Martens, flannel shirts tied around their waists, and rubber bands for bracelets. Most of them come from families as wealthy as the kids' at Dorrian's, but they dress as though they live on the streets. They go to the clubs to see up-and-coming bands play, bands who emulate the Ramones and Black Flag. Such a scene might be easier for me to fit into. I know about the pain and rage that threads through that culture. In many ways, though, I don't want to claim it. I want to be here, in this world of gloss and greed. I don't want to wallow in my anger. I want the façade. I want to be somewhere where girls can be girls, in high heels and dresses – the costume of male desire. Even if I'm not as stunning as the girls who surround me, I'm used to feeling like I'm not enough.

We stay most nights at Dorrian's until two, sometimes much later, and the next morning we drag ourselves out of bed and into the shower for school. We are often late, and I find myself in the front office, making up some excuse. I stay alert through the morning until Algebra II, which comes right after lunch. My eyes droop, my head feels heavy. I attempt to hide behind my text, full of the variables and equations taught in class, but which I haven't been awake enough to understand, as I give in and rest my head on the desk. I wake half an hour later, startled, a small pool of saliva near my mouth. Another teacher might not stand for it, but Mr. Hansen doesn't seem too bothered about student behavior in his class. He coaches lacrosse and spends his free time with the popular boys in my grade. Everyone knows he has a crush on Lori, one of the blond girls in that group, because he told a fifteen-year-old boy he considers his good friend, and that boy told everyone else. Even if he hadn't, it is obvious by the way he looks Lori up and down like he owns her whenever she's near.

The tenth grade has two popular groups. One is made up of the blond girls. These are the "good" girls who get superior grades, play sports, and drink wine coolers at parties. They are all indeed blond. Some of them are really brunettes but dye their hair to keep with the reputation. They spend time with the popular boys who play lacrosse and soccer and drink beer. The other in-crowd is made up of the Rachels. Amy told me that before I transferred to the school, this crowd was bigger, but slowly it whittled down to three girls, all named Rachel. They are still peripheral friends with a few others, but the Rachels have a stronger relationship, one that looks tight and exclusive from where I sit. It's no secret they know about things I know about too, like cocaine and pot, boys, and drinking. At lunch I watch them talking and laughing, and I feel some regret about my friendship with Amy. I allowed her to swoop me up, away from any other possibilities. I would have liked to get to know the Rachels.

Amy, sensing my longing, gets pissed at me often. If I'm late or don't call when I say I will, she won't take my calls and will ignore me for a few days. She grabs my hand if I try to change the station on her car radio.

"You don't touch my car without asking first," she snaps.

Once, she locks me out of her house, and I have to go to her neighbors to ask to use the phone to have my dad come pick me up.

Another time she leaves me at a diner with no ride home because I spent too long talking with some class-mates in another booth.

She tells me her neighbor, who is also her friend, liked me when she met me, but she thought the hairy moles on my arm were gross.

I begin to learn there are certain things I shouldn't tell her. Like when we meet boys at Dorrian's and I give mine a blow job, or the time I messed around with a boy in the back near the bathrooms. Amy wants to be intimate with boys too, but to her this kind of conduct is slutty. I suppose it is. She, like most girls, including the Rachels, has a different relationship to boys than I do. She engages in sexual acts with them if she wants, but from my vantage point it looks like she can take them or leave them if they are not just right. She considers whether she actually likes someone before she jumps into bed with him. She isn't wracked with anxiety when there aren't any boys around. And she doesn't need them to live, which is what it feels like for me.

Or at least this is what I assume, that I'm the only girl who feels this way.

I also don't tell her about my friendship with the new history teacher. He is young, fresh from college, no older than some of the boys Amy and I hang out with at Dorrian's. He is the faculty advisor for the yearbook, which I have joined in order to have something on my résumé for college. At the meetings, he is all business, assigning tasks to each of us. But when I find him in his office, and it is just the two of us, things are different. He becomes relaxed, flirtatious. He compliments my hair or my shirt. He laughs at my jokes. I like his attention. Soon I start going to see him almost every day after school, even when we don't have yearbook meetings. I tell him about Dorrian's and some of the boys there. He asks me lots of questions, and after a while our conversations turn to sex. We discuss blow jobs and virginity. We talk in explicit terms, using words like "cock" and "cum." When I leave, I feel tingly and light, high on attention. On weekend days, driving around with Amy or my dad, I try to determine where his house is. He told me the general area, and I fantasize about surprising him there some night, dressed the way I dress for Dorrian's, in short skirts with no stockings. Perhaps this is why he never tells me exactly where he lives. Perhaps he fantasizes about the same thing.

Many Sundays I'm still asleep when Mom calls. I sleep heavily. Tyler tells me when I'm up that she came in to wake me for the phone call, but I was so out I didn't budge. She looks at me suspiciously. I know what she's thinking. She thinks I'm sleeping off a hangover or I'm stoned. That's not it at all. It's just I'd rather sleep through the days so I'll be awake for the nights, when the boys are out.

"You don't know what Dad did," she says to me one of these Sundays. I've come down our hallway to use the bathroom after watching TV with Dad. She calls me in to her room.

"What?" I stand at Tyler's doorway. The Cure croons from her record player, the voice tortured and sad. Her room is baby blue, the color she chose when we first moved in, but someone wrote "we are the dead" in black marker over and over again around her doorframe. I have to assume it was her. Clothes I know she bought at Fiorucci and Canal Street Jeans litter the floor. She wears her hair short and spiked lately, and she draws black lines around her eyes. She must be a part of that downtown scene, the one where kids jump around in mosh pits, getting out their aggression. I shift uncomfortably. She's my sister, but I don't even know her. I don't know how she really spends her time, locked away in this room.

"Remember Harriet?"

I nod. Mom's good friend from art school.

"She jerked off Dad. Right in our house when Mom was home so she would find them."

"Mom told you this?" I say. My voice squeaks when I do. That familiar combination of jealousy and relief that our mother chooses Tyler as her confidante sits just beneath my skin.

"He wanted to be caught, the coward. Rather than just face her and say he wanted a divorce."

"Shut up."

"I don't know how you can hang around him." Her voice is bitter, full of hate that belongs to Mom, not her.

"I don't know how you can stand *her*," I say.

I walk away, annoyed, deeply bothered. I don't want to have this conversation with Tyler. About how Dad's terrible and Mom's great. She can choose to be brainwashed by

Mom if she wants, but I don't have to. For me, Mom is an unreliable narrator of our lives. When she speaks of my childhood it is always of the same three instances. The first is of me as a toddler. With my new grasp of language, she tells me again and again, I waddled into the living room, rolled on the floor, and said, "Tickle me." "You were such an affectionate child," she says wistfully. The next story is how she chose a Montessori school for me at two-and-a-half, and soon after starting I learned to tie my own shoelaces. The teachers often sent the older kids to me to tie their shoes if they were busy with something else. The final anecdote she tells is about when I didn't want Mom to cut my hair when I was five, so I went up to the bathroom, found the scissors, and cut it myself. Mom says she tried hard not to laugh when I showed up in the kitchen, my hair butchered. "I wanted you to feel competent," she makes a point of saying.

Her stories are probably true, but they are carefully constructed to build a happy childhood for me, one where I am just fine and she is a caring, considerate mother. One that can make up for the divorce, and for the fact that she left us. What she doesn't realize is her stories point to my willfulness, the ways I was able to lord my power over the world, and over her. She wanted me to be competent, sure, but I don't think she accounted for the possibility that I would match her competence at controlling our relationship. She pushes, I pull. She pulls, I push. This has always been our dance.

Really, Mom and I both look to stories to gain a sense of control. I believe Mom tells her stories so Tyler and I will accept and forgive who she is; she wants this more than she wants the truth, while I most want the truth. But what if I am wrong? What if Mom believes her memories as fiercely as I do? What if my memories are merely constructions like hers?

I pee, then go back into the living room. Dad's there, his eyes glued to the TV, some movie we're watching on HBO. I sit on the couch, too aware of him there, my father, who did this cruel, lascivious thing. He laughs at some funny dialogue, then stands.

"I'm getting a soda. Want one?"

I nod and watch him go to the kitchen. I decide to ignore this ugly thing about him. Who would I have left if I were to hate him the way I hate Mom?

◆ ◆ ◆

NORA'S APARTMENT IS on the Upper East Side, just eight blocks from Dorrian's, and Amy and I join Dad when he stays there on the weekends. Nora has two kids, a boy Tyler's age and a girl four years younger than me, and we all get along well. Jack is kind and smart, and sometimes he comes with us to the bar. He doesn't care about what I do there either, which is a relief from the judgment I feel from Amy.

At Dorrian's, Amy and I meet more and more guys. One of the regulars in his blue school blazer approaches me one evening, and I spend the night making out with him in a booth. Another night, an older boy brings me flowers, and we go back to his parents' three-story brownstone to have oral sex. Each time, I give my phone number, embarrassed by the New Jersey prefix. No one ever calls. At first this stings. But over time I adjust. I smirk when a boy says he'll call. I don't look at him next time we're both at Dorrian's, assuming that's what he prefers. It's just how things work in the bar scene. Boys and girls come together, and then they move on to the next. I want a boyfriend, but if I can't have that, I'll take this stand-in. It's satisfying somehow – the hopeful waiting, the flirtatious exchange, and then the rapt, sudden sexual attention. I begin to enjoy the immediacy of gratification. I still feel let down later when it is over and I am left alone, but this doesn't keep me from going back for more.

One night, after we've come back to Nora's apartment, no boys having taken the bait, I sit awake in the living room, watching TV. I can't sleep, and a John Hughes marathon is on, with *The Breakfast Club* just starting. I've seen all these movies at least four times. Dad and Nora come in. They were out with Nora's friends. He relies on whatever woman he's with to provide him with friends. He tells stories of friends from the early days with my mother, like the one about the two friends from Mom's art school who brought blow-up dolls as dates to a wedding. Or the guy Dad did mescaline with and then they couldn't eat the spaghetti the friend's wife served them because chewing felt like the weirdest thing in the world. If it weren't for the women in his life, I'm not sure Dad would have any friends at all. I don't know what happened. He used to be so popular, according to his high school stories. Somewhere along the way he must have lost confidence.

Dad wears a stern look on his face, but Nora is happy, her movements loose. She flops down beside me and lights a cigarette. She smokes 100's but only halfway. There have been times I was craving a cigarette enough that I smoked her crushed-out butts.

"What are you doing awake, honey?" she asks. I smell alcohol on her breath.

"I don't know. I can't sleep."

"Maybe you need to take something."

"No," Dad says. He stands at the entranceway. Something is bothering him. "She doesn't need anything. She just needs to go to bed, and so do you."

Nora rolls her eyes at me. "What, is he my father too?"

She laughs, but I can tell by the look on Dad's face that I shouldn't laugh back.

"He's right," I say. "I'm going to bed."

I get up and head to my room, unsure what to think.

◆ ◆ ◆

IT'S THE SUMMER of 1986 and Tyler's preparing to leave for college. I come home to hear Tyler in Dad's bathroom.

At first I don't think much about it – maybe she needs something in there we don't have in our own bathroom – but as the minutes pass, an anxiety starts rustling in my stomach. I go hesitantly to the door and listen.

"Tyler?"

I hear a glass clink, then something falls to the floor. That day years earlier with the Tylenol sits like a shadow in my mind, how I did nothing to save her. I press my lips together, trying to quiet my heart.

"What?" she finally answers.

"You OK in there?"

"I'm fine," she says. "I'll be right out."

"You sure?"

"Yeah, I'm fine."

I go back to the living room and sit on my hands on the couch to wait. My eyes are on the door to Dad's room. I think about calling someone, maybe Dad. Nora. If I have to I could always call 911. Finally, she comes out, looking the same as usual, just more tired. Spiky hair, black clothes. Her eyes look sunken beneath her glasses. She moves slowly, like she always does, as though navigating her way carefully through a world of hidden mines.

"Hey," she says, seeing me watching her. She doesn't quite meet my eyes.

"Hey," I say. I think about asking her what she was doing. I think about saying something, something about Mom's absence, Dad's preoccupations. Something about how she must feel really alone. Like me. But we don't talk like that. There's an unspoken understanding: I am Dad's and she is Mom's, and we are not to cross that line.

"I have a bad headache," she tells me, perhaps seeing my concern.

I nod.

"Aspirin wasn't working, so I thought I'd try something Dad has."

"You sure you're all right?" I ask carefully.

"Yeah." She smiles now, not a genuine smile, but a smile meant to tell me not to worry, a smile that says I should butt out.

I bite my lip, unsure whether to believe her. I want to say something, anything that will keep her from going away again to where I can't reach her. Not that I am reaching her now, but at least we are on the rim, our heads just above the surface. At least we are exchanging words. Seconds pass. She stands, I sit, trying to think of something worthwhile to say.

She raises her eyebrows. "Are we done here?"

I hesitate, and then I nod. I don't know what else to do. I watch her small body head back down the hallway and into her room. Eventually I hear her music come on – Sonic Youth or the Cult or some other band I can't relate to. I take a breath and turn on the TV, deciding to believe everything is fine.

At Nora's, Jack has friends over often. One, his closest

friend, tells Jack he thinks I'm cute. His name's Greg, a nice-looking guy with light eyes and a scar on his face from stitches he got after a fall when he was a child. He smiles often, and he's nice to me in a simple, straightforward way. I'm not used to it. I expect with boys to have to unpack their comments, read underlying text. I've learned at this point not to trust the things they say. Greg's kindness, though, is uncomplicated.

On nights when nothing else is going on, I fool around with Greg. His kisses are gentle, his hands soft. He asks me if I like what he's doing. I let his hands wander and go where he wants. In general, though, I feel bored. At the time, I don't know what it is. I feel itchy, expectant, like I'm in a permanent state of waiting. When Greg and I kiss and dry-hump, I feel empty, frustrated. I want something else, something more. And because I can't identify it, I decide what I want is to lose my virginity. And Greg, with his sweet, safe nature, is the perfect person to lose my virginity to.

One night, as we are kissing, I ask him why he hasn't tried to have sex with me.

Greg sits back and leans on his elbow. When I look at him up close like this, I feel a little turned off. "You're a virgin," he says.

"No, I'm not."

"You're not?"

"I haven't done it in, like, a year," I tell him. "But I've had sex."

Greg watches me. "So, you want to have sex?"

I nod. "Do you have a condom?"

"I'll find one," he says.

He jumps up to go, I assume, to Jack's room to find one. I take off my clothes, get under the covers, and try to gauge how I feel. *I am about to have sex*, I think, and I wait for a bodily reaction. When I was younger I expected I would lose it to someone I loved. Every girl did. It would be with a long-time boyfriend. I would have strong feelings about it. But lying here now, I find that's not true. I look down at my body, the white expanse of it. I feel almost nothing. Just a low-lying numbness. Greg comes back with a condom and gets under the covers with me.

"Whoa," he says, seeing I'm naked. "You move quickly."

He takes off his clothes, already hard. He goes down on me, and I close my eyes, letting myself focus on the feeling, letting myself go. Then he puts on the condom and pushes his way inside. It is uncomfortable, but not painful. There is no popping or searing sting like I'd read about. No fireworks or meaningful moment. I stay still, waiting for him to finish. He moans, and then he pulls himself out of me and flops onto his back.

"Nice," he says. He pulls me against his chest, and I lie there, feeling his heart beating quickly beneath my ear. I have no sense we are "one," as the cliché goes. I have no sense of anything. Just an emptiness. A disappointment. And that's it.

For two more weeks, I have sex with Greg. I held off having sex before because I had the notion I would wait for love. I wasn't sure I'd ever be loved, and I was tired of waiting. If I can't have love, I'll take the next best thing – or at least the thing I figure might get me the love. So now that I did it, I want to get good at it, and I assume practice will get me there. As soon as I feel I have reached that point, I break it off with Greg.

I don't tell Amy any of this. I don't tell anyone. I know initiating the loss of my virginity is a major faux pas for a girl. Girls can't make choices like that. If a girl has sex when she's drunk or overpowered, she's not considered promiscuous. But if you're aware of what's going on, it's this consciousness that makes you a slut. Losing my virginity is a choice I make. What's more, I orchestrate the whole thing, and I use a boy in the process. If that's not being a slut, I don't know what is.

◆ ◆ ◆

AMY AND I meet two guys at Dorrian's a few weeks later. We know who they are before they approach us. Most everyone does. They are part of a party production team in town, a group of guys who put together club parties where underage kids can dance, drink, and do drugs. Thrilled, Amy and I flirt like crazy, and within an hour, the four of us are in a cab, heading to one of their homes. The taller boy is Ben; the dark-haired one, Dave. They are both smart-asses, making comments about our clothes, our hair, and, of course, New Jersey, the whole ride there. But we don't mind. We can be smart-asses too, especially Amy with her sharp tongue.

Ben's home is an unbelievably huge loft on the Lower East Side. The ceilings must be twenty-five feet high, and one whole wall is a window. The Manhattan lights twinkle and wink, a whole world of people living their lives while we're in here with Ben and Dave. Ben turns on the stereo — Tears for Fears — and we follow him to the stainless-steel kitchen where he gets out four glasses and a bottle of whiskey. He pours each of us a shot. I don't want it. I don't like the burn of liquor in my mouth, and I'm always afraid I'll vomit trying to get the shot down. But I take it anyway, and while the others down their shots, I take a prim sip. I do my best to hide my grimace.

Soon, Ben and Amy disappear, and Dave guides me toward the black, contemporary leather couch. We kiss, and he peels off my shirt, his shirt, his jeans. He undoes my bra, hikes up my skirt, slips a hand between my hip and my underwear. I look at the windows as he slides them down. Our bodies reflect there. It is beautiful almost, the curves of our bodies connected. I can do this now, I think. I can let him in this far. This is what I wait for every night: a face hovering close above mine, his breathing fast and out of control. Him wanting me, all mine. He kisses my neck, my collarbone. So sweet, I can almost believe he loves me. And then he is inside me. He moves, gripping my hips and butt. Like he needs me, too. Our skin comes together and apart, growing slick with sweat. I wrap my arms around his back, holding on.

And then it is over.

He pulls his body away, the air suddenly cold. He pulls on his jeans, runs a hand through his dark hair, and goes off to the bathroom.

I turn again to see my reflection in the window. I am lying on the couch, alone, shadowy. A corpse. I quickly pull on my shirt and underwear. I fasten my bra beneath my shirt. I hear Dave in the kitchen and turn to see him pouring more whiskey. He holds a glass toward me, and I shake my head. I ask instead for water, which he brings me. That's nice.

When Amy and I leave that night, Dave hugs me then chucks me under the chin. It is sweet, affectionate, a big brother's gesture. I smile, not knowing what else to do. I guess this is just how it is. Having sex is lukewarm, something you share for an evening. It's friendship-building. What else should it be?

In our cab heading uptown, I tell Amy. I'm not sure why. I guess if this is going to be a regular thing, which I know it will be, I don't want to be so alone with it. I realize I'm going to need a friend. But Amy is aghast.

"You had sex? You didn't even know him." She stares at

me, incredulous. Her open window whips her dark, thin hair into her face.

I bite my lip. I don't know what to say. "It's not like he was my first," I say.

"What was he, then? Your fifteenth?"

"Ha ha," I say, though I know she's not trying to be funny. "It's not a big deal, OK? I lost it to Greg when we were seeing each other. I just thought it was time."

She turns away from me, eyes straight ahead. "It's a big deal to me."

I shrug, hurt. "That's your problem. Besides, what were you doing with Ben that whole time?"

She looks right at me. "Kissing," she says. "He took my number."

I shrug again, trying not to reveal my envy. "Lucky you."

She doesn't say anything more, and neither do I.

But I keep having sex with strangers.

One day, we wake up late at Nora's and find Dorrian's Red Hand is in the newspaper. Jack brings it to show us. A boy and girl met there, left together at four thirty a.m., and went to Central Park, where she was found strangled by her own bra two hours later. Amy and I read, our mouths open. Robert Chambers and Jennifer Levin. We know who they are. We saw them leave together the night before after Robert's then-girlfriend had broken up with him, jealous about other girls, including Jennifer. Robert is the tall, handsome boy we had watched from afar, one of the boys always in a blazer and topsiders. Jennifer was one of those tiny-waisted girls. They were regulars, part of the wealthy in-crowd. Amy and I both thought Robert was hot. His dark hair, the way he kept half his button-down shirt out of his khakis. He seemed so likable with his affable smile. But the article painted him in another light. Robert had been kicked out of a number of preparatory schools, and he had recently been expelled from Boston University for stealing and for hosting a party in his dorm. His lawyer claimed Robert didn't need to force anyone to have sex with him. Jennifer had been the sexual aggressor that night.

Amy and I take showers. We eat some breakfast. We try to go about a regular day. We talk about Robert Chambers as a badass, the reports of him having yelled obscenities in the street and then torn up the summons he received from a cop. We discuss the claims that he was kicked out of one boarding school after another for his defiant behavior. Inside, we are both shaken. Things have changed for good. Looking for guys in bars is suddenly not quite so innocent, and my having lost my virginity makes that even truer.

In the evening, we head to Dorrian's, hoping to talk to others, but there's a new bouncer at the door, and he shakes his head. Media attention, he tells us. The owner got in big trouble for all you underagers. Don't bother coming back. We go to a nearby diner, upset.

Over the next few months, the Robert Chambers murder, or "Preppy Murder," will build national attention. The story grows daily. News critics will write incisive features about wealthy parents leaving money for their kids on the kitchen's granite countertop as they run off to second homes in St. Barts. The parents are from the sixties hippie generation, grown up and bringing in serious cash, but still partying and rebelling. Their children grow up taking on adult behaviors – drug use, casual sex, bar hopping – without the wherewithal or guidance to handle them. Jennifer's death will come to represent the wasted lives of socialite idle youth. The focus will also be on Jennifer, painted as a sexual vixen who knew what she was doing that night. Robert's lawyer falsely claims she has a "sex diary," full of sexy tales and phone numbers. Robert claims Jennifer raped him. He and his lawyer claim Robert and Jennifer were having "rough sex," she wanted him to strangle her, and Robert didn't realize his own strength. A home video leaks showing Robert and a few of the beautiful girls from Dorrian's right after his trial. He pulls a head off a doll and utters the words, "Oops, I think I killed it." A clear connection in the media is made: If Jennifer wanted sex, she deserved to die. This stops me. It's not something I want to think about too much. So I watch the news, scour the papers, looking for more information.

In my mind, the Preppy Murder further equates sex and desperation. It shows I'm not the only one who brings my aching wants to sex. They are inexorable, bound together in a tight knot. I imagine Robert and his anger, his frustration like mine. I imagine being the one lying under him, wrestling with his passion. The one beneath his strong hands, his desire. I can picture the two of them in the bar that night, Jennifer with her pretty, tamed hair and unassuming clothes, somewhat different from those perfect girls I envied. She was more down-to-earth. More like me. Robert wore his gleaming smile, walking from table to table. Had he ever come to Amy's and my table I would have gone with him in a second. I would have held his hand in the park, as I imagine he held Jennifer's. I would have allowed him to push me into the deep, damp grass, to wrestle off my clothes, to bite at my neck. I would have pulled him against me, into me, deep inside to that silent, painful spot. Before I remember she is dead and gone, I will think how much I would have liked that, to meet him there at that place.

Five

LOSING MY VIRGINITY changes Amy and me for good. Maybe she sees my carelessness and doesn't know how else to express her concern. Maybe she's jealous of how easily I can relinquish my body. Maybe she thinks I'm like Jennifer Levin, putting myself into dangerous situations for no reason she can see. Or maybe she just thinks it's shitty that I have sex with people I don't care about and who won't care about me. I'm not sure. But I see it as my opening to get out. When school starts up again, I go to a party and make my way toward Rachel A. She's the prettiest, the one most boys at our school would like to get. She's also the quietest. She has a feline quality, sleek and slow-moving. She stands now with a beer in her hand, her legs crossed, one finger twirling in her hair. She looks bored. I prepared for this.

"Want to do some coke?" I whisper.

She turns to me, her eyes wide and sparkly. I can see my plan is going to work.

"You have coke?"

I nod. I took it earlier from my dad's drawer, which he has kept refilled since that party a few years back.

She smiles. "Let's go to my car."

We head outside and onto the street. The night is still warm from the summer. Dark leaves rustle from oaks that stand majestically in front of the house. I don't even know whose party we're at. She unlocks her car, and we get in. I file this: Rachel A is not so rich as to have a Beemer or a Jeep Cherokee like most of the kids at our school. Like me, she has to come from enough money to go to our school, but maybe not as much as the others. She takes a CD case from the door cubby, and I dig out the packet of foil from my pocket.

"Here," I say, handing it to her. "You can do it."

She opens the foil and smiles. "This looks nice."

"It's my dad's," I tell her. "Which means it's going to be really good."

She dumps some of the chunky powder onto the CD case and pulls a credit card from her wallet to break it up. "Your dad does cocaine?"

I nod. "He has so much, I can take this amount and he'll never know."

"Very cool." She keeps chopping with the card. "You're Kerry, right?"

I nod again.

"Why haven't we hung out before?"

I smile, feeling great. "I don't know."

She slices the powder into lines, takes a twenty from her wallet, and rolls it, just like the dollar bills I used to find rolled in my dad's apartment before we moved in together, back when I didn't know what they were.

"Your shit," she says, handing me the CD case and the bill. "You get the first line."

I take it from her and, using the bill, sniff in the thinnest line. The drug is sharp inside my nostril, and immediately I feel a course of lightning through my body. Razor-sharp, quick, bracing, like I've just plugged myself in. I give it back to her, and she snorts quickly. She dips a fingertip – nail bitten, I see, just like mine – into the edge of the powder and rubs it on her gums.

◆ ◆ ◆

A SUNDAY. MOM calls. She's been back in the States for a few years now, living in Chicago. I sit on the leather couch in the living room and pick at a hangnail. She tells me about seeing Tyler in her new dorm room, how she thinks Tyler's thriving there. Last time Tyler called she said she had a boyfriend. *A boyfriend.* My withdrawn, matronly sister. I told her I was happy for her, but really I was seething with jealousy. How can she have a boyfriend when I don't? What is so wrong with me?

"And you?" Mom asks. "What about you?"

I look at the rows of pictures on the entertainment

stand. Tyler and me as children. Dad and Nora on a recent cruise. Most of the photos are outdated, from when Tyler and I were much younger. Dad's many electronics and all their wires clutter the stand – the large TV, two VCRs so he can copy *Nova* and war-footage videos, all the stereo equipment. Our apartment is always cluttered, old computers and their parts heaped in corners, mounds of mail that's never been sorted, and the living room is no exception. Since hiring an interior designer when he first bought the apartment (one whom Mom claimed he was sleeping with), he has allowed the place to go to hell. Dad pays a cleaning lady from Nigeria forty bucks to come once a week, and she does our laundry, dusts and vacuums, and cooks us meals that she seals in Tupperware and puts in the fridge. Without her, I guess, we would live like bachelors, eat cereal for dinner, let laundry pile up in the hallway. Mom's apartment, by contrast, is like a wonderland. Like Dad she has lots of stuff, but hers is all valuable and carefully arranged. Local artists' colorful work lines her walls, bizarre sculpture juts from corners. She has an installation in her dining room, rows of tiny blue kites illustrated with clouds that flutter and wave when there's a breeze. It's a minuscule version by the artist of an installation actually hanging in Chicago's Museum of Contemporary Art. Every item she owns, from toothbrush to kitchen whisk, is a piece of art. She likes to say it's because she wants to surround herself with beauty, but her need for unique and beautiful things has always struck me as excessive, maybe even frantic.

"Kerry?" My silence makes Mom uncomfortable. She doesn't want to know how I'm really doing. She would never approve of the way I spend my free time, chasing boys and partying. If she could have her way, I would be like Tyler, waiting at home for her calls.

"I'm good," I say.

"No more parties?" she asks. There's a familiar edge in her voice, the one that's there whenever she mentions Dad. "Your father isn't leaving you alone while he goes off on business anymore?"

"God, Mom," I say. "That was ages ago."

"It was a few years ago. I hope your father's learned something."

I sigh. *He doesn't talk about you*, I want to scream. *Why are you still talking about him?*

"Can we drop this?"

"I have a right to an opinion when it comes to the parenting of my children."

"Not when you're not around to parent them yourself," I blurt and immediately regret it.

She goes silent, her code for feeling hurt. I close my eyes, wishing for once it were my feelings that mattered here. *I'm the one who got left*, I want to say. But her silence warns me against saying anything more. I can't stand her, especially when she's like this, but I still need her. She's my mother, after all.

"I'm going to go," she says in a tight voice.

"Fine," I say.

We hang up, and in the silence I hear a small moan from behind my father's closed door. I get up, march down the hall, and slam my bedroom door.

❖ ❖ ❖

AMY SEES ME laughing with the Rachels during lunch. I never say anything directly, but she gets the hint and begins to keep her distance. We say hello in the hallways. We talk briefly. There is no blow-up or tantrum, as I feared there would be last year. It turns out Amy is accepting, as though all along she knew I would leave our friendship.

I make friends with the Rachels' peripheral friends too, especially Tanya. We share a sense of humor and a love for pot smoking. And soon, as spring arrives, I find a boy. Heath, Tanya's boyfriend's friend from another town. Heath is round-faced, funny, and gregarious. He is just OK-looking, but he is one of those people whose personality is so great and his confidence so strong that he is magnetic. Heath sees me first at a party. Tanya tells me about it on the phone, excited at the idea of it, her and Jeff, me and Heath. We'll have so much fun.

Two weeks later, the four of us go together to a party. Heath makes jokes, trying to impress me. He watches me with admiring eyes. On the ride back from the party, people pile into the car, leaving little room, so Heath pulls me down on his lap. He holds his arms around me in a hug. I feel light and breathless. Elated.

The next day he calls me, and the next and the next. He goes on a vacation with his friends to the Bahamas, and he calls from there, too.

"I miss you," he says.

I grip the phone, letting myself feel this, a boy missing me, wanting to be with me. The truth is I don't miss him. I barely know him. We saw each other once since the night of the party. We made out on my bed while Jeff and Tanya were in the other room. It doesn't matter. I like the idea of him, of what he will be for me. So I tell him I miss him, too.

When he comes back he brings me a woven leather bracelet he bought at a stand on the beach. I put it on, loving it without question. It's proof he thought of me, he likes the idea of me, too.

Finally.

A boyfriend.

We have sex for the first time that night.

When I tell the Rachels, Rachel C, the one I connect with the least, the one who frightens me with her harsh, cutting laughter, says, "I appreciate you telling me first, but I'm fine with it."

I don't say anything, confused.

"We only went out for like a week."

"Oh," I say. "Good."

She flips her curls back and makes a face.

"He annoyed me pretty quickly."

I nod, unsure what to say.

"Some stupid comment about how he liked I knew how to drive stick."

I nod again. He made the same comment to me, except I had liked it. It made me feel sexy and powerful. I didn't tell her that.

"He says stupid stuff sometimes," I say.

She laughs, that mean, high-pitched laugh. "If you can stand him, I wish you guys the best."

I laugh too, hating myself for laughing. Hating I can't be myself with the Rachels, I'm so bent on being one of them. This is one of the reasons I like Tanya so much. She doesn't care what the Rachels think about her. If she were in my shoes right now, she would tell Rachel she likes Heath just as he is.

Tanya comes over after school and we get high in my bedroom. I shut the door, but that's just a courtesy. My father knows I smoke pot. He doesn't care. Once he even joined me and my friends in the living room as we passed around a joint. He had walked in the front door, and everyone froze. But he just introduced himself, and then asked for a hit. When he went into his bedroom afterward, my friends were in awe.

"That's so cool," one said.

"My dad would fucking *kill* me if he saw me smoking pot," said another.

"And yours smokes with us?" This one shakes his head. "Dude. That's awesome."

I smile and nod, but lately I'm thinking sometimes I'd rather have a dad who would kill me for smoking, who would never smoke with my friends. Having a dad like mine can make me feel out of control and anxious, like I'm standing on a high wire hundreds of feet aboveground. It makes me feel like no one will catch me if I fall.

Heath and I talk on the phone often, and on the weekend he and I get together with Jeff and Tanya. We laugh and listen to music. We go out for dinner and to the movies. Sometimes, Dad is home and he jokes with us in the living room. One time he even brings out a joint for us to share. Later he tells me how cute Tanya is, with her long blond hair and her adorable figure. When I tell Tanya, she jokes I'll come home one day to find her and my dad in bed doing bong hits.

"Shut up," I say, laughing. But really, I don't think it's funny at all.

Once Tanya, Jeff, Heath, and I go to a Japanese restaurant where the chef chops and cooks the food on a burner on the table, and Heath is so hysterically funny imitating the guy that I laugh hard enough to choke. At the end of each night together, Heath and I get alone and have sex.

We begin to build our own private jokes. Like once, after sex, we go to my kitchen to get water. We are quiet, careful not to wake my dad. He pours the water from the dispenser on the fridge, and then he turns on and off the little light in there.

"Isn't that cool?" I say. "I love the way that light looks."

From then on, whenever we go to the kitchen, he says, "Let me get the light," and he turns on that stupid little light on the refrigerator.

Another time, after a great round of sex, he asks me what I'm thinking.

"I'm thinking I just had a fucking religious experience," I tell him.

From then on, we call sex "going to church."

I am sure I've never been happier.

Only once do I go to Heath's house, and only after much cajoling from me. I take my sister's old Honda and arrive in the afternoon after school. I park and ring the doorbell, but no one comes. I listen for footsteps, watch the doorknob, willing it to turn, my heart beating too fast, that old rush of nervousness moving from my feet up my body. The uncertainty. *Has he decided he is done with me?* A cry makes its way from my stomach to my throat. Then I think I hear something. Talking. I walk down the front steps and listen. Yes! Heath is talking on the phone! He's in the backyard! Relief floods me as I see him there, lying on a lounge chair, facing the other way.

"Welcome," he says when he sees me.

I smile, trying to look nonchalant. Like I wasn't just on the verge of tears. I want badly for him to kiss me, to hold me in his arms. I want to yell at him. He knew I was coming, why wasn't he listening for me? How could he let me feel like this? Everything unsteady and angled.

He hangs up the phone, but he still sits there. It's a nice day, one of the first warm, sunny days of the season. Irises and daisies blossom on the other side of the yard. I know his parents are divorced and he lives with his mother and younger sister. But he doesn't talk about them. Even that information I had to wrench from him. Many times, I find, I feel like I just did on his doorstep, knocking at the door, waiting for him to let me in.

"Aren't we going inside?" I ask.

He frowns slightly. "It's so gorgeous out," he says.

"I want to see where you live."

He looks off into the yard where his cat is chasing a flying bug and laughs. "She never catches anything," he says.

"Heath," I whine.

He looks at me. "Oh, all right." He stands and I follow him to the back door. He moves slowly, leaning down to greet another cat lounging on the back porch. "We don't have much money," he says as he opens the door and steps into the kitchen. "Don't expect much."

I laugh. "I don't care about that."

He walks me through the small kitchen and den and up stairs that are carpeted with brown shag. "Come on," he says when I stop to look at pictures of him and his sister as little kids. There's a hint of anger in his voice. We go up another flight of skinny stairs leading to an attic room. Half of it has a twin bed and fish tank. His clothes are scattered on the floor. The other half has an easel splattered with paint, rags, and a card table covered with tubes of oil paint. He explains his mother paints on one side, but the other is all his. I sit on his bed and smile, wanting him to join me. He's acting weird and distant. I need him to touch me, to get close, inside me. I need to know he's still mine. He starts to pick up his clothes from the floor.

"Forget those," I say. I take off my shirt and dangle it over the floor. "I'm only going to mess it up again."

He hesitates, but he looks at my chest. I straighten my back a little, pushing out my breasts. I smile again. He drops the clothes on a chair and comes to me. It's so easy like that sometimes to get what I want. We have sex, using a condom. When it is over we lie together a moment. I bury my nose into his neck, smelling his scent. A car beeps, and Heath jumps up, pulling on his boxers, and looks out the open window.

"Denny," he yells. "What's up?"

"We're going to Riverside," the friend yells.

"I can't, dude," Heath says. He gestures back toward his

bed, and me. "I'm busy." He laughs, and Denny laughs too.

"Ah, OK, dude. I got it."

I smile, liking this, being the object of Heath and his friend's attention. Being the one Heath has sex with. When his friend leaves, though, Heath doesn't come back into bed. He starts pulling on his clothes. I get up and do the same, figuring it's what he wants.

When we get down to the second floor, I ask to use the bathroom. Heath points to it.

"It's small," he says uncomfortably.

I go in and close the door behind me. The bathroom is indeed tiny and cluttered. There's a brown stain in the sink. But I don't care about that. Why does he think I care so much? I pee quickly and flush, then run the water and wipe my hands on a damp bath towel. He's in his mother's bedroom when I come out, but when I join him he quickly makes for the stairs again. He waits at the door.

"You better go," he says. "My mom's going to be home soon."

"I'd like to meet your mom."

He grimaces. "Maybe another time," he says. "I've got a bunch of homework."

I nod. "OK."

I wrap my arms around his neck and kiss him.

"I'll miss you," I whisper.

He pulls away first. "I'll catch you later, OK?"

In the car, I try to shake off the feeling he's going away. His words echo in my head. *Maybe another time*. There will be another time. He said it himself.

◆ ◆ ◆

SINCE I CAN'T be with Heath as much as I would like, I fill the rest of my time with friends. I go to one of the Rachels' houses and do cocaine or we sit in the smoking sections of diners and drink coffee for hours. Rachel B and I, it turns out, have many of the same interests. We drive together up Route 9W to Nyack, New York, a small, artsy town that has cute little shops full of goods made by local artists. We buy beads and handknit hats. We gossip about people at school. She has a boyfriend too, a cute Filipino boy a grade below us, and we exchange stories from our relationships. She's been seeing her boyfriend for close to a year, so her stories are more dramatic, funnier. They have a lightness to them I can't get to with Heath, aware as I am of this constant nagging feeling he's about to end things with me. But I keep this to myself, laughing along with her when I talk about the weird way Heath doesn't want me lingering in his house.

With all the regular sex I'm having, I start thinking about birth control. Until now, I know, I've been lucky. Only once or twice has a guy not initiated the use of a condom, and usually only because there were none around. I am rightfully scared about pregnancy. After one of those condomless nights with someone I barely knew, I was terrified I was pregnant. When my period came a few days late, I promised myself I would never ever do that again. But I did, leading to another pregnancy scare.

I'm afraid of pregnancy, but I'm not really afraid of STDs. I should be. This is the eighties, when AIDS has begun to destroy person after person, taking them down as if with a machine gun. One of my mother's good friends has been diagnosed as HIV-positive, and another is already dead. But in the eighties, adolescent girls aren't afraid of such things. AIDS is relegated to gay men and IV drug users. It will be a number of years before females, and then African-American teenage girls, become the groups with the highest rate of growing AIDS cases. Being a young girl, I don't think STDs can touch me. I assume, as many teenagers do, I am impervious to diseases like herpes and chlamydia. Those things just don't happen to people like me. I'm more concerned about getting toxic-shock syndrome from tampons. Media hype has convinced me this is the thing to worry about.

It's the pregnancy worry that makes me call my mother one evening. She's doing her residency now in gynecology in Chicago. She'll be able to get me what I need.

"The Pill?" she asks when I tell her why I called. "You're having sex?"

"I have a boyfriend," I tell her, defensive. I sit cross-legged on my bedroom floor. I assumed telling her would

be no big deal. She's the one who pushed all those books –
What's Happening to Me? and *Our Bodies, Ourselves* – on
Tyler and me when we were younger. She's the one who
told Tyler and me, too much actually, that sexual feelings
were normal and healthy and even nice.

"I just want you to be careful," she says.

"That's why I want the pills."

"Not just that kind of careful, though," she says. She
hesitates, and I wait, a sick feeling starting in my stomach.
"Boys don't like girls who give it away too easily."

I set my mouth. "I told you, I have a boyfriend. We've
been together for over a month."

But inside, that sick feeling spreads.

She doesn't say anything.

"Forget it," I say. "I'll just go to Planned Parenthood."

"You should get an exam anyway."

"To look for diseases?" I ask. I feel like I might cry.

"Everyone should get an exam before going on birth
control."

"I thought my own mother might help me out," I say.

"I want to help." Her voice is calm and steady. She's using
the tone she gets when it's obvious my feelings are growing
out of control. It's patronizing and fake, and it's one of the
reasons I usually hide my feelings from her. "But I would
never prescribe pills without an exam."

When we hang up, I feel like I might throw up. I go to
the kitchen and down a glass of water. I dial Heath's

number, but it just rings and rings. Then I go to the living room and flip on the TV. I do anything. Anything to get away from the fact that my own mother assumes I'm easy.

◆ ◆ ◆

TANYA GRABS MY arm and pulls me into the student lounge.

"You got me in trouble," she says.

"What are you talking about?"

She sighs and looks around, making sure no one else can hear. "Heath told Jeff you did it doggie-style with him," she whispers.

I bite my lip, embarrassed. "So?"

"I won't, and now Jeff is saying if *you* do it with Heath, then I should too."

"We only did it once like that," I tell her.

"You know how they are," she says.

I do. All the boys in Jeff's crowd are obsessed with anything concerning sex. One ripped off a tag from an airplane life jacket that said "jerk to inflate," and he wore it in his fly for the day until a teacher made him take it off. They all have this ongoing joke about doing it from behind. They answer every question that way: "What are you doing?" "Doggie." "How would you like that prepared, sir?" "Doggie." They think it's hysterical, but we girls roll our eyes. "That's so *canine*," we tell them, which makes them laugh even harder. Now, though, I've been caught. Now Tanya knows my rolling my eyes has been a bunch of crap. I think back to the time Heath and I had sex like that. I didn't particularly want to. But Heath begged, and wanting to please him, I did. The whole time I hated it, how impersonal and dirty it felt, as though I could have been anyone beneath him.

Later, I call Heath.

"Why did you tell him?" I ask accusingly.

"I don't know," he says. "That's what guys do. Haven't you ever heard of the locker room?"

I take a deep breath, frustrated.

"You didn't seem to care when my friend was outside that time and I let him know we were having sex," he says. "I would say you even liked it."

"Fuck you," I blurt.

"Fuck you too."

I close my eyes, wanting to get us back to how we were. I'm not really mad at him. I'm mad at myself, that I do these things and then pretend I don't. I spend half my life lying about who I am and what I want. I don't even know who I am most of the time.

"Listen," I say. "Let's just forget it, OK?"

"Whatever," he says.

But I can tell he's still annoyed.

The next time we talk, he tells me he wants to break up.

I sit on the floor of my bedroom, my body empty, my heart wrung.

"Why?" I plead.

"It's just not fun anymore," he says.

"We can make it fun again." I close my eyes, knowing I sound desperate.

"Kerry," he says. I grip the phone, holding on to my name, his voice saying my name. "It's over." He wants to get off the phone, be done with it. He and his friends call having a girlfriend "dealing," and now he doesn't want to deal anymore.

"Can we at least talk in person about this?" I ask.

He sighs. "You can come here now, I guess."

Twenty minutes later I park the Civic in front of his house. Before I have a chance to get out, he comes out the front door and slips into the passenger seat. Keeping me away from his home again. My heart is pounding, my mouth dry.

"What did I do?" I ask.

He leans his head back against the seat, revealing his pale neck, his Adam's apple. I wish so much he would just gather me in his arms, but I know that isn't going to happen.

"I just wanted to have some fun, you know?" he says.

"We were having fun."

"Yeah. But things changed. You're starting to sound like me, do you know that?"

I stare at him, confused. "I am not."

"You are," he says, a million miles from me in the next

121

seat. "You say 'dude' and 'baked.' Those are things I say. And you make your voice do the same things mine does. I don't like it. You just want too much."

I lean back, that sick feeling spreading through my body. The feeling of being seen, exposed. My ugly needs giving me away once again.

"I'm over it."

I nod. I get it. My wanting makes me unlovable. It's something I already know.

"Let's just say we had a nice time and move on," he says, and smiles. This doesn't bother him at all.

My throat is tight with despair, but I smile back. We hug and he gets out of the car. I watch him go up the stairs to his door and disappear inside. He doesn't look back.

At home, I put on Roxy Music and listen to the song "More Than This," wanting the song to make me cry, but it doesn't. The music only lodges the sorrow more deeply inside. I go to the bathroom, and on the counter are the pills I finally got from Planned Parenthood. I just started my first pack, and in a month Heath and I would have been able to have condom-free sex. Stupid me, thinking it would last that long. I look at myself in the mirror, my flat, brown hair, the freckles sprinkled across my nose. I have never hated myself more.

The next morning I stay in bed, not wanting to wake up. The morning turns to afternoon, and at some point, Dad knocks and opens my door.

"I'm sleeping," I say, and turn over. I pull the covers over my head.

"It's two o'clock in the afternoon," he says. I listen as he walks to the bed. He pulls back the covers a bit and gets in beside me. "What's the matter?"

"Nothing's the matter," I say. "I'm just sleeping." I can smell his familiar scent so close. He puts his arms around my middle, like he used to when I was little, when we would cuddle together while watching TV. But I'm older now, and it feels weird, so I try to pull away. He holds tighter.

"Mmm. You're so warm and nice."

"Get out of my bed," I say, kicking him off. A panicky feeling is making its way through my body. I'm only wearing a T-shirt and underwear. I don't want him touching me like this, my father in my bed.

"What," he says, "I can't show my daughter a little affection?"

When I don't say anything, he gets up.

"Jeez, you're an ice cube."

He shuts the door and I let out my breath.

◆ ◆ ◆

TWO WEEKS LATER, Tanya, Jeff, and I go to a party. I know Heath will be there, so I dress as sexy as I can. A miniskirt, a tight-fitting top. I take a curling iron to my hair. When we arrive, he's flirting with one of the blond girls from my school. Jealousy seeps through my skin like water, but I try to act nonchalant, like I'm fine, like I don't need him so much. But as the night wears on, and as he drinks more and more, I grow frantic. Finally, I approach him.

"Come home with me," I whisper.

He winces. He can barely look at me. "I'm staying at Jeff's tonight." His breath is sharp from beer.

"Fuck Jeff's," I say. "Come with me."

He looks around, stumbles.

"I'll make it worth your while," I say.

He turns back to me, his eyes blurry from the booze.

"Drive me to Jeff's," he says. "His parents are away."

I scramble to find Tanya and Jeff and convince them to leave. And soon, Heath is in my car. He pokes at the radio, looking for something he likes as we follow Jeff and Tanya. I try to think of something to say, something that will endear me to him, get him back to who he was in the beginning. But when I look over at him, his eyes are rolling back in his head. I shake him awake when we get there.

Inside, he ignores me. He finds himself food, then turns on the oversize television to play a video game. I follow him from room to room, my throat tight, until finally he leads me upstairs to Jeff's parents' bedroom.

"Look at this fucking room," Heath spits out.

It is massive, with a king-size canopy bed. I know Heath struggles with this, with the fact that all his friends live in huge, luxurious houses while he lives in his simple home. He cares too much about it, like how I care too much about what people think of me, especially boys.

His mouth is tart and clumsy, and he yanks off my clothes in a hurry. He feels different, angry or annoyed. I don't know what. But I let him keep going. He pushes himself inside me. I was going to tell him about the Pill, but he doesn't get a condom anyway. He just pushes and pushes, jabbing and hammering, like I'm nothing beneath him. That blond girl, maybe. Or no one at all. Tears come to my eyes.

"Come on," he yells when I don't respond. "What's the problem?"

I look away, tears streaming.

He pulls out of me quickly, not done, and runs into the bathroom where I hear him retch.

I roll over and wrap my arms around my bent knees.

When he comes back, he lies on the other side of the bed and falls fast asleep. I sit up and see my clothes on the floor. Twisted shirt and crumpled skirt, my underwear rolled into a ball. I gather them up, my throat dry. I know I should leave. It is the only dignified thing to do. But then what? I'll be home, alone in my room, unable to sleep there, either. I think about the next morning, waking up with this ugly night weighing on my mind. The thought is simply unbearable. So I settle back down and wait for sleep to come.

In the morning, I wake to the sound of Heath in the room. He has put on his jeans and he sits at the end of the bed with his head resting in his hands.

"Don't say anything," he says when I sit up, "or my head will split open."

I put on my clothes, which I realize I cuddled with all night, and I get out of the bed. I'm thinking about how he said I want too much, and I'm desperate to get out of there, to prove him wrong, even though I've just proved him right.

"Do you need a ride?" I ask as softly as I can.

"I'll get Jeff to take me home." He doesn't even look at me.

I wait another second, but he doesn't say anything else.

For a brief moment, I see myself as though from a distance: my wrinkled clothes, my mussed hair, mascara smeared beneath my eyes, waiting for something from this boy who is done with me. I am pitiful, wretched even. I need to end this for myself. But in the same instant, the vision is gone. I wonder now if I had been able to maintain that perspective for maybe a few moments longer, perhaps I wouldn't have kept going down this path. Perhaps this would have been the turning point, the place where I learned my lesson and found a way to love myself. But my desperation was too strong. It was like a tidal wave, pulling me deeper into its current. And the rest of me was not strong enough to fight it.

Six

THAT SUMMER, MY dad rents a house on Fire Island off of Long Island. Fire Island is a small beach community made up solely of boardwalks, docks, and water taxis. No cars are allowed. In the summer, the towns on Fire Island come to life. Wealthy Manhattan families take ferries there every summer weekend, many of them leaving the children with nannies for the week when they have to head back to work. Two towns are renowned for being a gay mecca, where men can meet each other and have sex along the forested boardwalks, no one wagging fingers or turning their eyes in horror.

Our house is in Dunewood, a family-oriented community with only a small grocery store and a kids' recreation center. We have the house for July. I'm excited both to be on this beautiful island and to spend the month with Dad and Nora. She's become a second mother to me, kind and generous and thoughtful of my feelings, the mother I always wished for. I like the way she makes light of things, such as telling us men are good for three things – paying, carrying things, and sex. Later, she'll amend this, adding "waiting" to the list. She calls Tyler and me her "almost daughters." She's joking, but it means a great deal, to have her think of us this way.

One evening when I was feeling lonely and dejected because none of my friends were available, she rounded up my dad and took us for Chinese and a Mel Brooks marathon playing downtown.

"Everybody needs New York when they're feeling glum," she told me during dinner, "and what's more New York than good Chinese and Mel Brooks?"

"You make it sound like being a New Yorker is the solution for everything," Dad said, serving himself sesame chicken.

Nora shrugged and gestured for him to put some on her plate. "A lot of times it is. We have the best of everything here, food, museums, music, shopping. Listen," she said when Dad looked doubtful, "you're lucky I even talk to you. You're from New Jersey."

I laughed. Even feeling blue, Nora always gets me to laugh.

Dad allows me to invite a friend to Dunewood for the month. The Rachels are busy with their own family vacations in Europe and St. Barts, and this makes me nervous. I still live in constant fear the Rachels will exclude me, or forget me entirely if I'm out of sight for too long. Since I can't invite them, though, I invite Ashley. Ashley, who was with Liz and me at that gas station so long ago. Ashley, who tried so hard to keep me innocent that night, but to no avail. Even though we've been at different schools, we've stayed loosely in touch, and she still feels like a sister to me, sometimes more than Tyler, to whom I rarely speak. Nora's like another mother, Ashley's like a sister. The truth is I go through my life trying to piece together the family I want, the one I didn't get.

On the ferry to Fire Island Ashley and I are giddy, in great moods. Dad, Nora, and her daughter, Miranda, are down below, away from the wind, but we opt to sit up top, our hair whipping around our faces. We can see the island in the distance, a beacon. There's something about the summer, tanned skin, bare feet, the ocean air. We smile knowingly at each other. The thing with Heath hangs over me like a winter coat, and I am eager to shake it off. I heard that the best way to get over someone is to get under someone else. That's exactly what I intend to do.

Our first day, Miranda makes friends with a few girls, and Ashley and I go with them to the beach, where the kids in town hang out every night. I meet a nice-looking guy, Ace, who attends a prep school back in the city, and before the night is through we head off together into the tall beach grass and have sex. The following night we do the same. And then he leaves Fire Island for the summer.

I haven't spoken with Mom in almost a month, and I

like it that way, keeping her at arm's length. I could do without the guilt, without the need to always think of her feelings, and to protect my own from her needs. Times with Dad and Nora are so different, so much more *me*. I don't have to keep up my guard. Like today, in the Dunewood house. Nora walks past the sliding screen that leads onto the deck. She's in flip-flops and a sarong, a white wine with ice in her hand.

"That Giuliani," she says, shaking her head and gesturing toward the paper Dad's reading. "He's ruining New York."

"Most people would say he's making it better." Dad smiles at her. He sits beside me on a patio chair, the paper unfolded on his lap. I'm on a chaise, rubbing SPF 8 on my legs.

"I'm with Nora," I say.

"That's my girl," she says.

"I mean, it's nice not to have to put on my wipers every time I come to a light so the homeless guys won't start cleaning my windshield," I continue, feeling adult enough to comment on this now that I drive. "You know what's weird, though?" I say, after a moment. "Where did all those guys go?"

Dad laughs. "You do have to wonder. Maybe now there's some island in the Hudson teeming with men carrying liquor in paper bags. They're all looking at each other between blackouts like, 'Where the hell are we?' "

Nora laughs too, but then she gives a fake pout. "I don't want a nice New York. I want my grungy, dangerous, graffiti-ridden one back."

"It's not the real thing unless you have to hide your jewelry inside your clothes on the subway," Dad says.

"And split your money into different pockets, so in case you get pickpocketed you still have some cash," I add.

"And avoid Times Square like the plague." Nora laughs. We join her.

I love hanging out with them.

There is another boy, Justin, who Miranda and her friends covet. He is adorable. He has shocking blue eyes and sun-kissed hair, skin the color of beach sand. I can tell he finds me attractive. At the dock, after a day of tanning and swimming, I smile at him. He smiles back. He is two years younger than me – a baby. I can feel Miranda and her friends watching our exchange. They are jealous, impressed. I relish this, so different from the powerlessness I felt when Heath and I were breaking up.

"You're Kerry," he says when he comes over.

I tuck my hair behind my ear. I know I got some color today, and I feel pretty. "How do *you* know my name?"

"Your little sister told me."

Miranda. I smile that she called me her sister even though our parents aren't married, that she feels this way about me.

"You're asking about me?" I say.

"Is that OK?"

I purse my lips. Up close, he's even cuter than I thought. His wavy hair falls into his eyes and he brushes it away with a hand. I imagine kissing him and immediately my heart starts to flutter.

"I suppose it's all right," I say.

He smiles and goes back to his friends. Ashley, who heard the whole thing, grabs my arm.

"Jailbait," she says, and we both start laughing, remembering the night at the gas station so many years ago.

But as I watch Justin now as he walks off with his friends, that old anxiety creeps up. Having talked to him changes things. I want badly to close the space between us.

The next day I find myself watching for him on the beach, and by the time night comes, I am eager to get back to the dock. Like with every guy I am interested in, his point of view takes over my own. As I put on makeup, as I pick out my clothes, I think, *What will Justin think of this? How will Justin see me?*

I close in on him as soon as we get there.

"Let's take a walk," I say.

We go to the beach. But rather than pull me into the reedy grass, as I expected he would, he climbs the lifeguard tower. I join him and we sit there, watching the thick expanse of stars.

"You can't see the stars in Manhattan," he says.

I smile. He's a romantic.

"It's beautiful," I agree.

I look at him, at his features lit by moonlight. This close he smells like ocean air and freshly washed clothes. I want him to kiss me, to touch me. Something, so I know I'm really here. He looks back at me.

"You should know something," he says.

I raise my eyebrows.

"I have a girlfriend."

"You do?" My stomach sinks.

"Back in the city. We agreed we could see other people this summer."

I nod. I try to think of something to say, something to keep him from thinking of this girl. This girl who isn't me.

"I'm just here to have fun," I say. I'm remembering Heath's words. *I just wanted to have some fun.* It's what boys want. I know this well. And what's better than a girl who wants the same thing? I could be the opposite to this girlfriend of his. I could be the one who doesn't want anything from him, the one he then winds up wanting more.

Justin smiles, believing me. "Cool," he says, as I figured he would. "That's what I'm here for too."

He kisses me. The magic words have worked.

For two glorious days, Justin and I fool around whenever and wherever we can. We are all over each other, our hands, our mouths, constantly seeking the other. My skin smells like his. And then, as with every boy before him, things start to get difficult. With Justin, it starts when I want to have sex and he doesn't. He won't. He claims he and his girlfriend agreed they would not have actual sex with anyone else. I do everything I can to lure him to break this promise. I move my hips against his. I push him down on the bed. I refuse to do anything to relieve him of his excitement except have sex. But nothing works. He is resolute, and this begins to affect my ability to stay patient with the boundaries of our relationship.

One evening, just a few weeks later, we are all on the dock when I see Justin about to get into a water taxi.

"You're going somewhere else?" I ask. "I thought we would hang out tonight."

He looks at me, at the desperation there, and I see I have ruined everything. I have exposed myself once again.

The next night he tells me he doesn't want to have that kind of relationship with me anymore.

As usual, I can't let it go.

The following weekend, Justin shows up at the dock with a friend from home. He's not a remarkable boy in terms of looks. Short brown hair, large nose and mouth. He brought beers and he passes them around with confidence like he's hosting a party. By this time, Justin is actively ignoring me. I know what he's thinking. I'm one of those crazy girls, the kind no boy wants. I am determined to prove him wrong. So I approach his friend, and his friend responds to my attention. Justin laughs nervously. He avoids looking at me. I am making him uncomfortable, and I like that. I want him to suffer, but more, I want him to think of me. To think of me with his friend.

As the night goes on, his friend puts his arm around me. He exchanges some words with Justin, and soon he and I walk off together. I look back to see if Justin is watching, and sure enough he is.

It's a beautiful night, the stars brilliant, the air still. Moonlight casts a silvery glow on the beach grass along the boardwalk. I hear the waves washing over the beach, that soft hush as they pull back. The guy pulls me by the hand to the back of Justin's house, where no one is home. We go in a back door and into a laundry room. He pulls me down to the floor, kissing me, his hands already in my pants. It doesn't feel good. His mouth is sloppy. He is moving too fast, but it doesn't occur to me to resist. Only once my jeans are off and he's rolling on a condom do I begin to feel the rise of shame, and then it's too late. He's inside me. And then he's done. I look down at my body. My leg is bent at an odd angle, like it's not mine. The hair down there is matted and dark. He is sitting near me, zipping up. I don't dare look at him. I grab my underwear and pants and yank them on, not wanting him to see my nakedness. This guy I don't know. This guy whose name I can't even remember.

Later, I walk back to my house alone, trying not to feel anything about what's happened. What's happening to me.

How I keep setting myself up. I am lightheaded, outside myself, the same feeling I had that morning with Heath at Jeff's house. Someday I will realize this is a necessary distance, a way to inure myself to the injury of what I've done.

I think instead of Justin, how he looked as I walked away with his friend. Only now, in my memory, walking along in the moonlight, do I see his expression. It wasn't jealousy or longing, as I told myself at the time. It was disgust.

◆ ◆ ◆

BACK AT SCHOOL that fall, I tell no one about what I did on Fire Island. After the Peter R episode, I got smart about keeping my sexual activity away from school. By the time I graduate, I will not have been physical with one person from my school except Peter, who has long graduated himself by then. Regardless of my actions, I know what it looks like for a girl to have so many sexual partners. No one likes a girl who so willingly opens her legs.

I learned this in fourth grade, when Ariel Devine developed early and kissed two boys under a desk. She was immediately branded as a slut. We were all embarrassed for her, this girl who had so little self-respect she would kiss two boys – *two!* – without any shame.

Ariel Devine. I remember her first and last names, yet I still can't recall the name of Justin's friend.

At my high school, we have our share of sluts too. Two

of them graduated the year before. They engaged in the standard fare of sleeping with random boys. I listened to the Rachels gossip about what they had heard. Kate slept with Seth and a month later with Keith. Sarah slept with Keith right after she slept with Danny. There were plenty of other girls who were having sex. None of the Rachels were virgins, and neither were most girls I knew. However, these girls, unlike Kate and Sarah, kept sex restricted to relationships. I gossiped along with them, but secretly I wondered why it was the girls' fault that the guy didn't want more than a one-night stand. For all the ways we were told girls had equal opportunities, all the evidence that we wouldn't have to struggle to have what men have, this double standard seemed intractable. If a girl had sexual curiosity – and what girl doesn't? – she was considered a ho. Boys could direct the course of their sexual development; girls couldn't. It was the oldest dichotomy in the world. And it was also terribly confusing. I didn't want to be a slut. No one does. But since I didn't seem able to hold on to guys for more than a few weeks, I didn't see any alternatives that didn't include stopping sex entirely.

I had other, less intellectual feelings about these rumors too. I wondered, for instance, why almost everyone other than me seemed to be able to have relationships. I could have sex. Oh, yes. But I could not keep a boy's attention beyond that. Thinking about this opened up a deep hole in my chest, one that seemed to have no bottom. The only answer I could come up with was that I, unlike these other girls, was simply not lovable.

In twelfth grade, we have just one slut: Jeannette P. She is the queen of all sluts. The sluttiest a slut can be. She has made her way through our entire school, stopping only at boys more than three years younger than her. Unlike Kate or Sarah, she is not popular. Nor does she seem to care. She is tall and muscular, with acne scars along her jaw. She laughs loudly and is unimpressed with most everything. She is a scholarship student at our school. The boys tell stories about her. She shaves her pubic hair into a Mohawk. She likes to be tied up. She'll give head for over an hour. We don't know whether any of it is true, but we know not to join in on the boys' snickering. Jeannette scares us. Her sexual power is too raw, too *there*. Worse, she shows no shame for it. It is as though she has taken this narrow list of options for girls – slut or virgin – thrown them out, and come up with her own. Like she's saying, "Of course you're going to call me a slut, but that's because you let yourself be bound. I, on the other hand, am not going to let anything stop me from having a good time." Her attitude is both impressive and terrifying, and no one knows what to make of it.

Like everyone else, I avoid Jeannette. But one afternoon, after speaking with a teacher about a project after school, I find myself alone with her in the parking lot. Our cars are the only ones left. Mine, the Honda Civic; hers a silver

Dart. Usually the lot is filled with Mercedes and Audis, typical for New Jersey private schools. I try not to look at her, just open the lock on my door.

But she calls to me, so I glance up.

"Can you give me a jump?" she asks in her hoarse, smoky voice.

I stare at her, not understanding.

"A jump?" She hits the hood of her car. "My battery's dead."

I'm still not sure what she wants me to do. I know how to drive a car, but no one has taught me yet about car maintenance. "I've never done that before," I say.

She laughs, that loud laugh. "Drive your car to this spot, and I'll do the rest."

I do as she says, and she pops my hood and attaches her jumper cables. Once she gets her car running, she drops my hood and thanks me.

For an instant I consider saying something to her, something about what's happening to me, or maybe about Justin's friend. But what I want to say has no shape to it. It's just an amorphous feeling, a sense she might release me from my loneliness and the ways I try to quell it. Besides, this is the first we've ever spoken. She probably doesn't even know my name. Anything I say will sound wrong, too intimate. So I just smile.

"No problem," I tell her.

When I see her again, passing in the crowded school

hallway, I keep my head down, relieved I never said anything.

◆ ◆ ◆

EVERY SO OFTEN, Tyler comes home from college. She doesn't visit often, since Mom is on the other side of town from her school and that's where she goes now, so when she does arrive, looking calm – happy, even – I eye her tentatively, an exotic animal moving through the apartment.

In the middle of the night on one of her visits, I get violently ill. I pull a blanket and pillow into the bathroom and spend the rest of the night on the cold tile floor, alternating between vomiting and restless sleep. In the morning, Tyler finds me. My father is not around, a common occurrence, so she calls the pediatrician and then puts an arm around me to get my weak body down the elevator and into her car. I hold a paper bag, in case I have to puke again, and lean back with my eyes closed. My mind is blurry and exhausted, but I listen to Tyler's soothing: "You'll be OK. The doctor will help you. You'll feel better soon."

On the way home, after learning I had food poisoning and getting antinausea medication, I do feel better. I glance over at Tyler, grateful, aware that simply being cared for makes me better. The doctor's attention, Tyler's kindness – these are the things I crave.

In the spring, I apply for college. Some of my friends, like Rachel B and Rachel C, are nervous about this impending change. They worry about leaving friends and family and, in Rachel B's case, her boyfriend. I am looking forward to getting away. The past few months have been torture because there are no boys. The parties I go to with the Rachels every weekend are filled with the same cast of characters, the same beer, pot, and cocaine. Drugs and alcohol don't hold my interest the way they do for many others. It's boys I want. Most boys in my school are in long-term relationships, or I know them too well to find them attractive, or I am too embarrassed to have the Rachels know I find them attractive. Worse, Heath shows up to some of these parties, and he is now dating one of the blond girls from school. I see him drinking a beer with his arm around her waist, and I feel worthless, a discarded piece of trash.

There are no boys. And when there are no boys, I get anxious and bored, like I am waiting for my life to begin.

I apply to five colleges, as suggested by my guidance counselor. I pick three, and he picks the other two. I am not attached to where I wind up, as I have no real aspirations at this point. I haven't thought enough about it, my mind always set solidly on boys. I think maybe I'll study English. This year I'm taking an elective called Minority Literature, and for the first time I have found myself between the pages of a book. Almost everything we read, from Carson McCullers's *The Heart Is a Lonely Hunter* to Louise Erdrich's *Love Medicine*, reveals characters wrought with loneliness and unfettered desire. In their pain I find a depth of feeling I cannot allow for myself. My own is too much to bear alone.

Dad takes Nora and me shopping. We try on piles of clothes, Nora encouraging me to buy things I'm unsure about. Dad sits on that bench, watching us enjoying ourselves, enjoying it himself. I don't know enough about Nora's financial situation. I know she lives in this unbelievable rent-controlled apartment near Gracie Mansion, and she has some family money from the oil industry. But Dad treats her the way he does me, lavishing her with clothing, jewelry, whatever she wants. I can't help but think of his parents. His father yelled at and demeaned his mother daily, while she twittered and accommodated whatever he wanted. Maybe Dad feels like he has to make this up to his mother by taking care of the rest of us. Maybe every woman is really just his mother in some way.

When the college verdicts come in, all three I chose reject me, and I am accepted by the two my counselor suggested. I decide to go to Clark University in Massachusetts only because the other one was my safety school. College isn't about the academics. It is solely about getting away, about having more freedom. Mostly it is about having access to a whole new crop of boys. Every change in my life is exciting and hopeful, an opportunity to start over, to shed my tiresome, needy self and become a lovable person. This change is no different.

◆ ◆ ◆

THE SUMMER BEFORE we all leave for college, two of the Rachels rent an apartment in Long Beach Island. They will be there for July and August. They invite me to come for two weeks of that time. I am honored, but also a little disappointed. I wanted to be included for the whole thing.

Mid-August, I drive down the Garden State Parkway, watching as the oaks change to pines and sand scatters into the highway edges. Seagulls call out. Summer, with all its promise again.

The apartment is in a weathered building about five blocks from the beach. The Rachels' rooms have full-size beds, but mine, the guestroom, has two twins. I hang my clothes in the closet, trying hard not to feel like an extra. My first day I walk down to the beach with Rachel A and dip my feet into the icy water. That is the last time I see the ocean while I am there.

That night we drive to a club that juts out onto the bay. The Rachels know a few of the guys, and around midnight we wind up at one of these guys' houses. There is beer and pot, and more important there is a boy I find attractive – a scruffy guy with black curly hair and thick, dark eyelashes. He's nice enough, and by the time the sun is starting to rise we are naked and tangled in a sleeping bag in someone's bedroom. I don't sleep until I get back to the Rachels' later that morning, and when I wake in the late afternoon, I find the Rachels have been sleeping all day too. We eat cereal, light up cigarettes, and drink coffee. And then we start all over again: drink some beer, go to a club, hang out at some guy's house, have sex with a nameless someone.

Except Rachel C's sex is with a particular someone. She has a boyfriend here. Rachel A also has some kind of ongoing drama with a boy. I am really the only one having random sex. Because of this, I urge Rachel C to call Heath. They are still friendly, and almost every weekend friends have been coming down to visit. If Heath came, and we were stuck together again in this tiny apartment, maybe I could get him back. Maybe I could be having sex with just one person again. So she calls, and to my delight he agrees to come in for a night.

He arrives that first Saturday. My throat clenches with desire when he walks in, tan and lanky. His charming smile, that body that used to be mine. Cocaine is available, which some of us are thrilled about, so we open up bottles of beer, light up cigarettes, and snort lines. After a few hours he goes out to see the ocean, and the Rachels and I sit cross-legged on the brown carpet to strategize.

"He has to sleep in your room," Rachel C says. "It's the only other bed."

"Unless he decides to sleep on the couch," I say.

"We won't let that happen."

"And then what?" I bite my nail, anxious.

"And then you lure him into your bed."

We smile. There's no question in our minds that this is all it takes. Men are so easy that way. If they have sex with you, they can be yours. Even though this hasn't been the case in the past, I still believe it. It's written across every ad, every movie, every love song. Sex equals ownership.

In the early morning hours, Rachel C shows Heath to my room.

"You can crash in here," she tells him.

He nods, uncomfortable. Until this point we were all just buddies. Now he was going to be alone with me. I brush my teeth and change into a T-shirt and sweatpants in the bathroom. When I come into the room he is already under the blankets and facing the wall.

"Are you asleep?" I ask as I get into the other bed.

"Almost."

I stare at the ceiling, nowhere near sleep. I hold the blankets against my chest and my heart pounds beneath my hand. Having him so close yet not near me is torture. I want him so badly. It is not a sexual want. I want him to love me again. I want to know I'm worthwhile. I take a breath.

"Heath?"

"Mm."

"You could come over here, you know."

I wait, my body buzzing with anxiety. My heart feels like it might explode.

"Don't you think if I wanted to I would?" he says.

I close my eyes, my throat tightening. After a few moments, I climb out of bed and go to the living room to have a cigarette. I can't sleep in that room now. I find Rachel C there with the TV on.

"The cocaine," she says. "I can't sleep." She cocks her head at me. "Oh, no. What happened?"

I tell her.

"Bastard," she says. "You don't need him." She says it loosely as she lights a cigarette.

She doesn't know that I do.

Heath leaves the next morning, the last time I will see him.

Two nights later, we have a party. About twenty guys and five girls on the island come to the apartment to drink and smoke. By this time, I have slept with three different guys, only one of them twice. But none of those boys are at this party. Around two in the morning, most everyone straggles out. Rachel C's boyfriend, who is drunk, stays behind. They go into Rachel's room, and I go into mine, exhausted. A few minutes later, I hear arguing, and suddenly he comes through my open door. He lies facedown on the extra bed.

I sit up in bed. "No way. This is my bedroom."

He doesn't say anything. Rachel C stands at the doorway, pissed.

"You can't sleep in here," she yells at him.

"Fuck off," he says.

Rachel turns to me. "I don't want you sleeping in the same room."

"This is my bed," I say. I consider telling her I am not remotely attracted to her boyfriend, with his big muscles and slicked-back hair, but I might insult her. "I was about to fall asleep. Get him out."

"I can't," she says, her anger now at me. He snores softly.

"Where the hell am I supposed to sleep?"

"The couch."

I grimace. "The couch? Where some guy spilled beer? Where everyone drops cigarette ashes?"

She shrugs, still mad.

"Forget it, Rachel. He's asleep. I'm about to do the same."

She narrows her eyes and stomps out. I hear her door slam. I don't want her mad at me. Our friendship is still way too tenuous. But I am so tired I can barely stay awake.

Sometime later, I am not sure when, I wake to the feel of the blankets being pulled back.

"What are you doing?" I try to push him away, but he is strong. He traps my arms on either side of me as he pulls off my underwear. I can smell him, old beer and body odor. I hear the TV on in the main room, which means someone is probably awake. I think of who that person might be, just on the other side of the wall, just a yell away. His T-shirt, which is cut into a tank, hangs down, brushing against my face as he rises up with athletic grace to pull off his sweatpants. Panic floods my body. I try to pull my hips away and close my legs, but he yanks me back and wrestles them open. The thought comes: *This cannot be happening.* Just as I think it, though, I become calm. Numb. The situation is also so familiar, the feel of my underwear sliding off my hips, a person I barely know hovering above me. I don't think of the word "rape." I won't associate that word with this moment for many, many years. Perhaps this is why I don't scream or yell out. I whisper instead, "Don't."

But he does anyway. His breath hot and fast on my cheek. His hairy legs scratchy against my own. Up, down, up, down. I hold my breath, willing it to be over, my mind empty. The TV in the other room drones on, whoever is watching it unaware of us here, of me. It doesn't matter. Why does it matter? It's just one more guy. Just get through it. All you have to do is get through it. After a bit I give up, letting him do what he wants. Up, down, up, down. Every few minutes headlights move across like a searchlight. Eventually he grunts and pulls himself out so he comes on my stomach. I keep my head turned away, my eyes on the shadows on the wall. I feel like I might throw up.

"You're a cool girl," he says before he goes back to his bed.

I say nothing. I think about crying, but I don't. Eventually, I get up to wipe my stomach with a towel.

The next day I don't tell Rachel. I don't tell anyone for many, many years. As far as I know, there is nothing to tell. I had sex again. This time with Rachel's boyfriend. And if she knew, I am sure she would no longer want to be my friend.

Seven

IN THE FALL, I head to college, leaving behind what happened in the Long Beach Island apartment, leaving behind what feels like a rash of mistakes and bad times. I am determined not to put myself in those situations again, although I'm also not yet sure how to do that. The new surroundings of college make me optimistic. My father helps me carry my boxes and duffels to my new room, and then I shoo him out. I'm ready to get started with my new life, that hopeful blank slate. This is the start of a new era for me, when I'll be confident and smart. I'll stop burying myself under my need. I unpack my brightly colored comforter and packaged toiletries. I set a new Brother word processor on the solid wooden desk, a gift from Dad, an unspoken vote of encouragement for doing well while I'm here. I don't tell him, but it means a lot to me, especially because of my interest in writing. Maybe he noticed.

I hang the tapestry I bought in Manhattan at a downtown flea market. It is blue and white, South American, and it brightens the cinderblock, white-walled feel of the tiny room. When my roommate arrives, she's pleased. She's from Ecuador, and the design feels familiar and homey to her. We're confident we'll get along just fine.

We're also happy because neither of us is anything like the other girls on our hallway. We congratulate ourselves on being more mature, more self-sufficient. We don't hang all over each other, anxious about being away from home. We aren't interested in having high-school-grade crushes or dramatic fights with our new friends. We've both done our share already, and now we're happy to be on our own, to start again. She has a group of Latin American friends she's met through the international students' orientation, so she doesn't need me in order to feel secure. Likewise, I have Zoë, a childhood friend of Rachel C's from back home.

Zoë lives in the other freshman dorm on the other side of campus. She's beautiful, with big blue eyes and butterfly-shaped lips, but she doesn't believe she's beautiful, and this makes her all the more endearing to me. Her roommate, from Rhode Island, is here on scholarship. She dresses differently from us. She feathers her hair, as though it is still 1980. She paints on too much makeup. But Zoë invites her to come along with us wherever we go. She doesn't judge her for these external things the way I do. Or maybe it's just that I want Zoë all to myself.

◆ ◆ ◆

"I'LL COME TO your room later," the guy says. A girl waits, annoyed, eyeing me up and down. I scribble my dorm number on a piece of paper and hand it to him. He stuffs it in his pocket and the girl whispers something to him. He smiles and regards me before turning to head down the stairs with his friend to the Pub, the campus bar into which I can't go because I'm only a freshman. David. His name is David. We met earlier at a party and kissed, and then he and his friend wanted to go to the Pub. I tagged along, hoping the bouncer wouldn't notice me, but he stopped me at the door.

I watch David go, a longing tugging at my throat. Zoë left the party early too. She wanted to call her high school boyfriend at his Pennsylvania college. There is nothing for me to do except go back to my dorm and wait.

I eat a few cookies from the care package Nora sent. Then I brush my teeth. I change into pajama bottoms and a tank top. I put on music. Midnight comes. Then one. Then two. Hollow, I finally fall asleep. Sometime later the door opens and I wake, my heart fluttering, but it is only my roommate, back from her night.

The next day, Zoë and I discuss David.

"Why are you wasting your time?" she asks, lying on her bed. I sit on the floor of her dorm room, drinking coffee. "He didn't come see you when he said he would. He's obviously an asshole."

"Easy for you to say. You have a boyfriend."

Zoë looks oddly at me. "How does that change David being an ass?"

I shrug. It just does. She has someone, I don't. In my mind, this makes her worth more than me. I lean back on my hands, breathing out, and say aloud the thing that is always right there, the painful thing that guides me so unsteadily through my life: "I want a guy to want me. To really want me."

"There are better guys here who can do that." She says it as though it is that simple. In her world, I'm sure it is. She reaches for my coffee, and I give her a sip.

The boy on Long Beach Island comes to my mind, his dark, shadowy face hovering above mine.

"I want it too badly, though," I say.

"You just haven't met the right guy."

I watch her, so confident in her logic. There are times I feel like I live in a different universe, as though I am watching other girls through a glass wall, these strange creatures who seem to know how to be loved.

"Give it some time," she says. "We've only been here two weeks."

I think of David, the way it felt to have his hands cradle my head when we kissed, the scratch of his stubble against my chin. All I know is I want that feeling again.

That night, early evening, while I am working on a paper, David shows up. He pulls me onto my bed and strips me down, takes out a condom from his back pocket. I am aware of the girls laughing and calling to one another in the hallway, aware too that my roommate could walk in at any time. In general, I feel no connection to these girls. They spent their first few weeks at college drinking for the first time and too much, winding up in the emergency room with alcohol poisoning. Their eyes widen with fascination at the mention of marijuana. Coming from sheltered lives, they gravitate toward being out of control, something that frightens me to no end. My roommate and I make fun of them as they steal baseball caps off the tops of boys' heads and run away giggling. We call them childish. We think of ourselves as superior. But I know right now, under David's thrusting body, there is nothing better about being me.

Afterward David says something about meeting friends for a late dinner, and he is gone.

I go to the bathroom to clean myself up. I remake my bed. I bring my paper back onto the screen. I do what I can to bring back normalcy.

The following weekend I see David at another party. He is with that girl again, the one who waited impatiently for him at the Pub. This time I notice a familiarity between them. She pulls something off his sweater. He pushes a curl off her face with his finger. They're a couple, a couple that allows hookups with other people. This is nothing startling at a college campus. Casual sex is part of the culture, as is sexual exploration. But as much as I'd like to be the kind of person who can go with it, as much as I hoped I would be, I feel betrayed. Joining college culture hasn't changed who I am.

When I tell Zoë this later, she laughs. "You weren't betrayed," she says. "He made it clear he wasn't going to give you anything more when he dissed you that first night."

To get my mind off David, I find another boy. Adam. Adam, with his lanky body and bright eyes. Adam, who laughs easily and who dances around the room without a trace of self-consciousness. We fool around in his house after a party, and then he walks me back to my room. Twice he calls me, which gives me hope, and then on my birthday he gives me red beaded earrings he bought at a street fair. I put them on immediately. I wear them every day. A week later, though, he stops calling.

Next is Dominic, who I meet on the boys' side of Zoë's dormitory hall. Dominic has a girlfriend at home with the same name as me. I know this, but I fuck him for a week anyway. We joke that if he calls out the wrong name, it really won't be the wrong name. I see him at the campus gym and that Steely Dan song plays over the loudspeaker – *I'm a fool to do your dirty work...* . We catch each other's eyes and laugh, but we don't have sex again.

Then Wes, Dominic's roommate. Once, Dominic walks in on us, but he just shrugs. "Getting my keys," he says. "I'll be out of your way in a sec."

It continues like this, each boy anodyne to the last. I try not to think on it too much.

◆ ◆ ◆

WINTER BREAK, I pack up my things and head down to New Jersey. As with all changes, I look forward to it, to the relief it promises to give me from myself. Snow, which was layered thickly on the sides of the Massachusetts Turnpike, all but disappears as I come back into the Tri-State area. Ugly, bare black trees are scattered in the landscape. Trucks shoot out thick bursts of black smoke as they merge into the slow traffic. I listen to music and smoke cigarettes, and out of boredom peer into other cars, looking for hot guys. I have a fantasy some gorgeous guy will see me, motion for me to pull over, and we'll begin a long and meaningful relationship. It never occurs to me that long and meaningful relationships don't start this way. But then, I have this fantasy just about everywhere – on a plane, in a restaurant, a bar, walking down the street. Someday, I figure, all the love songs and movies will be right, and love will find me. I do not understand at this point that real life is nothing like this.

Dad isn't home from work, and the apartment is quiet. I leave my bag packed on my floor and call the Rachels. I do not yet have the eerie sense, as I will in later years, that this is no longer my room, my stuff. James Dean posters still hang on the walls. The jewelry box on the dresser is stuffed with necklaces and bracelets I no longer wear. The bookshelf is packed with books from high school English classes and yearbooks. I don't yet have the urge to look through my things with wonder as though they aren't my own. For now, I feel I still belong here.

I leave Dad a note and go to Rachel A's. Her parents are divorced, and her father, who has remarried, left town for the holiday and gave her the keys to his house. We're psyched.

When I arrive at Rachel A's, Rachel C is already there, and we talk about our colleges, what it's like to be home from college now, how different life feels. Rachel C tells us about how cool her roommates are, and how they are already running the freshman class. I laugh and nod, but I'm aware of the old feeling I have with the Rachels, of how smoothly they seem to own their lives, while I stand awkwardly outside my own. I want to believe college has changed me, made me more confident, but here now with the Rachels, I see everything is the same as before.

Soon, two boys come. One I recognize. A long time ago, when we were in third grade, we were friends. His name is Charles, and he and Rachel A became fast friends at college when she learned he dealt coke. The other one, Will, is Charles's friend from high school. He and Rachel have been sleeping together for the past week. Nothing serious, she tells me while they are out buying beer. Just having fun. Rachel, I have come to realize, is one of those girls. She walks with confidence. She says whatever she wants without having to run the words first through her mind, trying them out. She really doesn't want anything more from boys but to have fun. She used to be anorexic, and she does cocaine almost every day. She definitely has her painful wants and longings, like me. But when it comes to boys, she would rather keep them at arm's length, out of her immediate space. This combined with her relaxed grace and beauty makes her immensely desirable.

I am so jealous I could die.

When Charles and Will return, we settle back onto Rachel's father's couch and lay out lines of coke.

"I remember now," Charles says to me. "You had that cool football game that vibrated and moved the little men around the board."

I laugh, remembering. We were eight years old. I had handed him one of those little men while we played that day at my house, and our hands had touched. It had been one of my first exciting moments with a boy, the electricity of our hands touching, the possibility in that spark. I don't recount any of that though, doubting it was the same for him. "We've come a long way from that football game, haven't we?" I nod toward the white powder on the table, and he laughs too.

Will glances between us. "You guys know each other?"

"We went to elementary school together." Charles

chops the powder with an American Express. "She was one of the few cool girls there."

I smile at Charles for that, and when I look at Will, he's looking back. Will has the same air of relaxation Rachel does. He knows he's hot. He can sleep with any number of beautiful girls. He pushes his long blond hair behind an ear and smiles at me, a slow, sexy smile. A smile suggesting more, and my heart quickens.

"Very cool," he says.

The next night, we do the same thing. And the next night, again. Once, Will and Rachel disappear into her bedroom, but they come out less than an hour later, ready for more lines. On our fourth night, we are all so cozy with each other, having snorted and smoked and talked so much, we lean against one another, piled into the bend of the sectional couch. I am enjoying myself. I belong, a part of things, here with the Rachels. I don't need a boy's hands on me, for once in my life. Until one is on me.

Will's hand, in the tangle of our bodies. He slips a hand beneath my leg where there is a hole in my jeans, and he runs his fingers along the exposed skin. Igniting my need, awakening that part of me. I glance at Rachel, but she doesn't see. Neither does Rachel C or Charles. It is between Will and me, our secret. His secret desire for me. I like that. And something else. Something I am less eager to admit. Rachel, for all her perfection, is not enough for him. But maybe I could be.

Around one in the morning, I put on my coat to go home, and Will surprises me by asking for a ride.

Rachel, who has just lit a cigarette, looks at him as he stands.

"You're not staying over?" It is a casual question, but I recognize the hint of worry in her voice. Maybe Rachel isn't as free as I thought. Maybe she sometimes feels like I do, waiting, always waiting for a boy to save her.

Will shakes his head. He doesn't hear her anxiety. Or else he doesn't care. He reaches for his army jacket. "I have to get home," he says.

"I'll call you tomorrow," I say to Rachel as Will follows me to the door.

We listen to music as we drive through the dark streets. I am so tired my body aches. A few hours ago I started refusing lines, knowing I needed to give my body a rest. I love the way cocaine makes me feel. It's the opposite of most every other drug I've tried, all of which made me feel out of control. Cocaine centers me. It tightens time, brings everything around me into sharp focus. Lots of people take drugs to loosen up. Not me. I want to be pulled together. I want to look around and feel that I know everything I see. Cocaine does this. It erases the questions. I feel confident, resolved, so unlike the unsteadiness I usually feel. When the high wears off, everything is blurry again. Uncertain. Worse, the only thing you want to do is sleep, and you can't. I had been unable to sleep until three or four in the morning each night, and then slept until noon. I was waking to have coffee and a bagel with Dad, then heading out to Rachel's again a few hours later. I was ready to take a day off, maybe go shopping with Dad.

Will directs me through the streets of Englewood, my high school's wealthy town, until he tells me to slow in front of a large, modern ranch.

"Thanks for the ride," he says. He clicks off the seat belt.

"I guess I'll see you back at Rachel's."

He nods, but he doesn't get out. I wait, the air growing thick between us.

"Well," he says. "Good night."

He leans toward me for what I assume is a good-bye kiss on the cheek, but his lips land on mine. I kiss back, and his hands go to my back, my waist, my legs. I put my hands in his hair, pulling him toward me. We pull apart and start to laugh.

"What the hell was that?" I ask.

"Oh, come on," he says, reaching for me. "It was bound to happen."

I smile.

"Take me home with you."

On the drive to my apartment, he keeps his hands on my body. He finds the hole in my jeans again.

"You wore these purposely to make me crazy."

"What are you talking about?" I laugh. I am high, no

longer tired. I'm not thinking about Rachel. No way. I'm not thinking at all.

We barely make it to my bed before our clothes are off.

After sex, he falls asleep beside me, but I toss and turn, unable to drop fully into deep sleep. I am too energized, overwhelmed by what I've done.

Late morning we wake, and I drive him home. He kisses me on the mouth when we reach his house.

"What about Rachel?" I ask.

"What about her?"

"Aren't you guys sleeping together?"

He shrugs. "It was nothing. She won't care."

It was nothing. Sex with Rachel was nothing. Maybe, after me, he doesn't want to do it with Rachel anymore.

I think of Rachel the night before, the way her voice went up just slightly when she asked if he was staying. "You can't tell her. She'd hate me."

He smiles, not bothered at all. "No problem."

I call Rachel later, just to force myself to be normal.

"You *have* to come back tonight," she says when I tell her I'm staying in. "It won't be the same without you."

I light a cigarette, the guilt digging at me. Will most certainly will be back there tonight, and this frightens me. Regardless of his use of past tense, I don't have any idea of his intentions, if he'll have sex with Rachel again now that we've had sex. I am smart enough to know it would be good for me to stay away, let Will wonder about me. But if I do, I know I'll wind up pacing the apartment and smoking, frustrated I can't control what's happening over there. Plus, Rachel's words feel good. Maybe I matter to her, to all of them. I blow out a long stream of smoke.

"OK," I say. "I'll come for a little while."

I don't want to think too much about Rachel after we hang up, so I wander out to the living room. Dad is there, smoking too, the TV on. I sit beside him.

"I haven't seen you much since you've been home." He stubs out his cigarette. The smoke sits in a hazy cloud above us. Someone is always smoking in this apartment.

When Tyler and I first moved here six years ago, I brought home a kitten from a friend's house. I didn't ask Dad. I knew not to. Dad had already made us give away our cat. Right after we moved her to a friend's house, she ran away, traumatized, and no one ever saw her again. I hated him for that, for letting Tyler and me lose our cat on top of everything else we lost that year. And I figured if I didn't ask, just let him see how cute it was and how much I loved it, he would let me keep it. But I was wrong. Dad didn't want a cat he said he knew he'd wind up having to take care of eventually. I begged to keep it, but Dad refused and he drove us to the pound to give it away. I wouldn't talk to him the whole way there. In the short time it had been living with us, it had developed a wheeze. I didn't think much of it until the man at the pound asked whether it was the cat or me breathing like that. I could tell by the man's expression he would have to put it to sleep. I screamed and cried, but Dad made me hand over the kitten. I figured the cat had gotten sick living with Dad's constant smoke, and I hated him even more.

Now that seems far away. I settle back into the couch, looking at the game he has on the television. "I've been busy," I tell him. "With friends."

"Why don't you have your friends come over here?"

I light another cigarette. I don't really want it, but I'm annoyed.

"Because," I say, "we want to hang out somewhere else."

He smiles, not catching my mood. "I like it when your friends come over. It's fun."

Dad thinks I'm proud when he hangs around my friends, trying to get laughs, telling me later which ones he thinks are cute, but it's embarrassing. Once, after he sat with my friends while they passed around a joint in the living room, I told him to get out and he pouted. Another time he came crawling into the living room on his hands and knees, just to be silly. I wish he would just leave us alone like a normal parent. I want to say, "Get your own damn friends," but what I say is, "Well, they're not coming."

His smile drops. "I'm just trying to have a normal conversation with you."

"Is that what this is?" I ask, smart-mouthed.

"You've got quite an attitude for someone who prances

through here just to eat and sleep." When I don't answer he says, "So glad you could come home for the holidays." And he leaves me there alone.

At Rachel's that evening I try to act ordinary. Having Will near me, knowing there is something between us, something no one else knows, is electrifying. We pass each other to go to the bathroom or get a drink, and the movement of the air between us makes my throat flutter. Our knees touch when we're on the couch. Our eyes meet every so often. The arousal is so strong, my guilt fizzles beneath it. I can't wait to get him alone, and I don't have to. I take him home again that night, and the next one as well.

"You're not going to sleep with Rachel again?" I ask a few nights later in my bed. I'm still amazed he's chosen me over her.

"Nah."

"Just me?"

He laughs, not at all bothered by the neediness I'm so bad at keeping hidden.

"Just you," he says, and pushes my knee, opening my legs again. I spread them willingly, thrilled.

Back at school, I tell Zoë. She listens wide-eyed and laughs, and I tell her she cannot tell Rachel C, no matter what.

"Why?" We are in her room, as usual, eating the chocolate-chip granola bars she and her roommate keep stashed in a desk drawer. She eats these instead of candy when she wants something sweet, but I know she'll probably feel bad about it later and make herself throw up. Sticking her fingers down her throat is apparently not new for her. She held off for the first few months, perhaps hoping to be someone different when she first got to college, like me. She is not secretive about it. Not at all. In fact, she urges her friends to join her. "It makes you feel so much better," she says. But I hang back in the room when they head down to the bathroom. I like the idea of controlling my weight, but puking doesn't make me feel any better, only out of control.

"I stole him from Rachel," I explain now. "They'll hate me."

"He wasn't her boyfriend," she says, opening another bar.

"That doesn't matter." I know I can't make Zoë understand the way it is with the Rachels. There's them, and then there's me. It's always been that way. "Just don't say anything," I tell her.

She shrugs. "All right."

But I wish I hadn't told.

Will and I speak a few times by phone, and I do my best to keep it light. Still, I push things just enough to make plans to see him at Columbia University over a weekend.

I drive back down to New Jersey, where Dad is away for the weekend, and leave Will a message from the apartment. I take a shower and do my makeup. I turn up my stereo to drown out the quiet. The old anxiety is with me, the feeling I'll be left here wanting, that he's changed his mind. But he calls back an hour later, and soon I am on my way into the city.

He meets me in the lobby of his dorm and we go to a party. Like the university, the party is far up on the West Side, not far from the Port Authority Bus Terminal where I went with Liz and Ashley to meet Milo all those years ago. We enter a building and take the elevator to someone's apartment. College students in cocktail dresses and button-down shirts fill the rooms. No one dresses up like this for parties at Clark. I stand on the sidelines in my jeans and cowboy boots, gripping a sweaty beer bottle that is lukewarm after half an hour. I do my best to act nonchalant, like I'm not uncomfortable at all. I watch Will chat with friends. He introduces me a few times, checks to make sure I'm OK. He's nice enough.

I want to get back to his room, though, where we can take off our clothes, all his attention on just me. *Just you*, he told me that time. I remember that, cling to it, as I sit on a brown, velvety couch and wait. When I told Zoë about us, I made it sound like we had something special, something that rose above the betrayal of Rachel. Our connection was irresistible. I told the story like a movie plot, like *About Last Night* where Demi Moore and Rob Lowe give in to difficult love, where, as much as they try, two people can't deny the forces that bring them together.

Finally, around midnight we walk back to his dorm. He and his roommate, who is conveniently gone for the weekend, sleep in bunk beds, and Will directs me to the top bunk. I go first to the bathroom, my eyes averted from anyone in the halls. This is a boys' floor. No one knows me, and I'm obviously here for one reason. I brush my teeth quickly and throw some water on my face, and then I rush back to Will's room. When I get there, he's lying on the bottom bunk. My stomach is hollow as I climb the ladder to the top bunk. I feel out of place, like I shouldn't be here at all.

After a minute Will comes up to join me and we have sex. He jams his hips into mine, moving like a jack-hammer. Was this what our sex was like before? I can't recall. I barely enjoy it. When he's done he climbs back down the ladder, leaving me there on the strange-smelling sheets in the darkness. He says something about the beds being too small, some apologetic comment, but his words make no difference. I can see I'm an utter fool.

Back at school, I hang around Zoë's room. I try to focus on my schoolwork. I get the flu and stay in bed for three days. I am sick, but more, I am sick of myself. Sick of my desperation and emptiness. Sick of the constant defeat. I am convinced if someone will just love me I will be able to focus on something else. I'll be able to enjoy my life. I'll feel whole and real, released from this weight.

One evening, I head down Zoë's hall to the boys' side.

Eli is in his room with a few of the other guys. I know Eli is attracted to me. I have thought about the possibility of liking him back. He's a good-looking, sweet boy from a little town in Maine. Even though I slept with half the guys on his hall, he never wavered from treating me with respect and kindness. But for some reason I can't pinpoint, I'm not attracted to him. Perhaps it's his kindness, which I am not used to. Or else I don't like the insecurity I see in him, too much like my own. Or maybe it's just the outdated way he wears his hair. Whatever it is, I am determined to push through it. I want to be loved, and Eli might be the one to finally do so.

I flirt with him, and by the end of the night we are in his bed. He is both skilled and tender as a lover, which surprises me. It is a nice night, a really nice night, but I leave the next morning without the crazy feeling I usually get when I like someone. As much as I want to, I don't feel drawn to him.

Two days later, Eli knocks at my door. He is flustered and upset, and he tells me he has some things to say. I sit on my bed as he pulls a piece of scrap paper from his back pocket and starts reading from it. How we had this night together and then I just disappeared. How we were friends first and this matters to him. How he wants to be closer to me but I don't seem willing to let him in.

I blink, put a hand to my mouth. No one has ever spoken like this to me. No one has ever thought of me long enough to write down notes about what they want to say. I reach for his hand and pull him down beside me. I kiss him hard on the mouth.

Eli and I date for the rest of the school year. We go to SweetTreats for ice cream, or we go to the Lebanese restaurant for falafel. We shop together at the health-food store for food. We spend lots of time cuddling on his bed watching rented videos, and his roommate sleeps in friends' dorm rooms to give us time alone. Everything is "we." I love to use the word. I make a point of it whenever I can. *We* saw that movie already. *We* can hang out with you Friday. I'm comfortable, almost content. This is such a new feeling, to be loved, no longer wracked all the time with wanting, no longer nervously searching for a boy. I feel for the first time like a normal girl. I'm happy and self-contained. I finally inhabit the other side of the glass wall.

There is another feeling, however. Somehow, I am not committed yet to the relationship. Eli is not enough. Before summer starts we decide we will visit each other as much as possible, but I am also hoping to see Will, maybe even Heath. I still want those boys I can't really have, and with Eli around the wanting feels more like just that – wanting, not need. It is as though he fills my hunger just enough to keep me from feeling ravenous when I go up to fill my plate at the buffet. This is selfish, I realize. What's more, it makes no sense. I've been claiming I want one boy to love me, which Eli is willing to do, yet now that I have it, now that I'm experiencing how good it feels, I won't step fully inside.

The morning after I get home to New Jersey, I have to leave for a cruise with Mom, her new boyfriend, my grandparents, and Tyler. I do not want to go at all, but like all things with Mom, what I want doesn't matter. The cruise is to celebrate my grandfather's eightieth birthday, and if I don't go, no one in the family would forgive me. Mom already considers me the selfish one.

I leave messages for the Rachels, anxious to have some fun before I have to leave. I know there is a party that evening where all of our high school friends can reunite. But strangely, no one calls me back. Finally, I get a friend, John, on the phone, and he agrees to drive out to the party with me.

When we get there, I see the Rachels. Everyone is in the big backyard, which has a cement patio and a fountain. I walk toward the Rachels, full of excitement, but they turn their backs and walk the other way. I stop, my throat closing.

Zoë told.

I get myself a beer and hug a few other friends. I feel nauseous and twitchy, unable to focus. I take a breath and head toward them again, this time making them stop.

"Let me explain," I say to them.

They wait, scowls on their faces. Rachel A keeps her eyes on the grass, not even meeting my eyes.

"I shouldn't have done it, I know."

Rachel C twists her mouth in disgust. "You lied."

"I know," I say. "I'm so sorry." I look at Rachel A. She's the one I need to apologize to most, but she still won't look up.

"We could never trust you again," says Rachel B.

I press my lips together, trying not to cry. That's when Rachel A finally looks up.

"I thought you were my friend," she says.

Tears pop into my eyes. I want to tell her I was her friend. I didn't want her to get hurt. But for all the ways I tried to make it OK, thinking she preferred to keep boys at bay, thinking she chose cocaine over intimacy with boys, thinking she could have anyone she wanted, I knew that wasn't true. I knew she needed to feel chosen just as much as I did. It was easy to romanticize what was happening, to make up some bullshit story about our love. The truth is, Will and I had nothing. Will was just one more attempt to fill my ugly emptiness, and this time it was at the cost of my friend. I hadn't thought of her at all. I was self-absorbed and insensitive. I cared about no one but myself. I close my eyes, knowing this. There is nothing I can say, nothing that will change the sickening truth of what I did. I'm as disgusted with myself as they are. The three of them walk away.

I find John to let him know he'll need to get another ride, and I speed home, crying the whole way. Back in the apartment I immediately call Eli, who tells me he's coming down to see me. I stay awake, smoking cigarette after cigarette, until he arrives at three a.m. and holds me until I have to leave for the cruise four hours later.

PART TWO

The Other Side
of the Glass Wall

Eight

WHERE BEFORE I felt tentative with Eli, I'm now fervent. I cling to him like a lifeline, like the only solid thing in a sea of sand. I've allowed every other valuable thing to pass through my fingers. My friendships, my self-respect, my relationship with my sister. Maybe Tyler and I are too different to be friends, but we shared a childhood. We survived together. I could have at least had a comrade. When I was a little girl I used to love animals. I used to whimper over every smashed squirrel on the road, outraged at human carelessness. I used to run in front of strangers on sidewalks, stopping them so they wouldn't step on an ant. "It's alive and you're alive," I used to exclaim, adamant in my conviction. I wanted to be a veterinarian, or maybe a wildlife biologist. I imagined myself comforting a dog as I pulled sharp burrs from its paws, or in the wild somewhere, like Jane Goodall, coming to know some special animal the way she knew chimpanzees. But somewhere along the way I let that go too, lost to boys. Everything lost to boys. I won't allow it again. Something has shifted inside me. Suddenly I see what I've done, the way I behaved with the Rachels, all those boys who never cared about me. I've been grasping at nothing, running in circles, trying desperately to fill the emptiness inside with nothing but air. If I think about it too much, I feel shame, so much shame. So I don't. I focus my thoughts on moving forward, with Eli.

I want to change, and I believe all I need to do is want that. I need only to love Eli. It never occurs to me that it's not really about him, not really about the boys. All I can think to do is to resolve: No more boys, no more grasping onto them as they turn away from me. I can feel the restlessness inside, the wanting always fluttering just below the surface, but I decide to ignore it. I can choose to turn away from my need, like so many boys have before. I don't want to own it anymore. Don't want anything more to do with it. I move to Maine that summer to be with Eli, and to be away from the ruins I've left behind in New Jersey.

Eli's house is small and simple, heated in the winter by a woodstove. Only in the past year, Eli tells me, did his father build stairs from the first floor to the second. Before that they climbed an old ladder to get to the bedrooms. Worn, knotted rugs cover rustic wood floors. The rooms smell like burning wood, even in the summer. I love the simplicity, the sparseness. I love the idea that a family doesn't need so much stuff to be whole, that perhaps there are other ways to feel full.

I also love Eli's mother. Susan is a painter who is studying to be a psychotherapist. She wears her husband's old shirts with jeans and almost always has paint on her hands. She cleans herself up only on days she takes her mother, who suffers from Alzheimer's disease, out to lunch. My own mother is endlessly concerned with her appearance, wearing carefully applied makeup, Ralph Lauren, and Manolo Blahnik, always seeking others' approval, even mine. I know it's wrong to compare them, that there's no point to it, but I do it all the same.

Susan paints daily. Some days she lets me enter her studio and see what she's working on.

"It's nice to have a girl around," she tells me one day after emerging from her studio. She puts water in the kettle so we can have tea. I take a seat at the table, happy to hear I'm welcome.

"Living with a bunch of boys is fun, but I don't think every woman could do it."

"They're smelly," I say.

She laughs. "True. They're also not talkers. This house can get very quiet."

"Except for the grunting."

She laughs again and I smile, loving that I'm making her laugh. "No one around here wants to hear what I have to say."

"I do," I say, and I mean it.

Susan is working on a series of portraits called "Kylie's Crow." Each one shows a crow in varying iridescent blacks, blues, purples, and greens perched on a tree outside a window. Kylie is a terminally ill girl Susan counsels each week, and Kylie tells her she sees a crow at her window every so often. The paintings are Susan's attempts at capturing that crow. As Susan recounts this for me, her eyes tear, and I am deeply moved by how sensitive she is to this girl, to the world's tiny details.

Once, Susan calls me to the window to see a fox in their backyard. I've never seen a fox before. Its fur is a fiery orange, its tiny nose twitching. We watch quietly as it creeps through the long grass.

"He visits us every so often," she tells me. "It always feels like a gift to see him there." Her face is lit up, open.

I understand entirely what she means, that shocking color of fur, the lightness of his step. It seems otherworldly that he is actually there, in front of us, letting us see. "He's beautiful," I say.

She smiles at me. "You're not a city girl at heart, are you?"

I shrug, unsure.

"No. You belong in the country, where you can be yourself."

I watch as the fox bounds back into the woods, realizing she's right, wishing I could live here forever.

Susan takes walks every day, and when Eli would rather

sleep off a hangover or watch TV, or when he's busy chopping more wood for the stove, I go with her. She tells me about her family.

"My sister once confessed she didn't know why I painted the things I did," she tells me. "She said good art is of landscapes." Susan laughs. "As though all the other brilliant work out there – Picasso and Degas, Jackson Pollock, Paul Klee – none of that is good art."

I laugh with her. I know some of those painters because of my mother, and I really want Susan to like me, to think of me as her equal. No one's ever talked to me like this, like another adult.

Susan walks on, quiet now. Sometimes when she grows silent like this I feel intrusive, as if despite saying it was nice to have me around, she actually prefers the silent house of men. After a bit, though, she continues. "It was a mean thing to say to me. Painting is my life's work. She basically said what I do is shit. My sister was so often thoughtless like that. Finally I had enough."

I think about my mother and the insensitive way she sometimes treats me. As though reading my thoughts, she says, "What about your family? You never mention them."

"I keep hoping if I don't mention them, they'll go away," I say, and she laughs. But I describe them, relieved to finally tell someone how difficult things have felt. She listens, nodding to let me know she understands.

"My mother used to paint," I tell her.

"Really?"

"Yeah, but it's different," I say. "She left it behind to be a doctor."

"Still," Susan says. "Your mother must know what it feels like to capture something – a moment, or a feeling. All people who make art want to express what's inside."

I consider this. It's hard to think of my mother this way, as someone who connects to her core. I feel disappointed, but I'm not sure why.

Susan glances at me, seeing my doubt. "You never know what's going on inside someone. When my mother developed Alzheimer's, she started inadvertently peeling back years of protective layers. She used to wear a hard mask whenever I was near, always keeping me at bay. Now her face lights up when she sees me. There's something beautiful in that, in the way something as terrible and destructive as Alzheimer's has given her a chance to be herself again, and us a chance to recover our relationship."

Susan has tears in her eyes and she doesn't look at me. I can see there's something else she's not sharing. Anger, perhaps, or a deep pain she has to protect. I stay quiet, not sure what to say, not sure what she wants from me.

"Enough about me," Susan says after a moment, shaking away the moment like a dog shaking off water. "Let's talk about you. Tell me about your interests."

I hesitate, stepping to the side as a car ambles slowly by.

"I guess I'm not sure yet."

"There's got to be something."

"There is reading," I say. I shrug.

"Reading is good. What do you read?"

I shrug again. "My sister sent me some novels I liked." I don't feel comfortable, like I'm trying to talk about something I have no knowledge of. So I'm relieved when she stops me and points to a dandelion that is twirling about, though there is little wind and nothing else around it is moving with the same force.

"Look at that," she says. "How can anyone not think there is some great energy in the world, propelling things?"

She says things like this often, making me think.

Susan makes us dinner most nights, but she refuses to do dishes because of her eczema. Somewhat proudly she shows me the inflamed, dry skin on her palms while Eli's father, a quiet, gentle man, stands scrubbing at the sink.

"Oh, please," Eli says, annoyed. "You could do dishes if you didn't aggravate the eczema with paint."

Susan doesn't look at him. "Eli has eczema too." She turns to him with her calm exterior, but I see that there's something more volatile brewing beneath. "I'm so sorry about that, honey." She reaches for his hand but he yanks his back.

"I'll live," he says.

Her face crumples, revealing things I didn't know but are suddenly clear – how much she needs Eli's love and approval, how insecure she really feels. She turns and walks from the room, but Eli doesn't seem to care.

◆ ◆ ◆

ELI WORKS SOME odd jobs, cleaning and repairing boats, painting houses. Some days, if it's something quick, he takes me with him. I sit in the grass in the sun with a book and observe. Eli is tall and muscular. He has ropy veins in his forearms and big, masculine hands. I love the way he looks, the size of him. When he hugs me, I feel safe.

One night he goes out with a friend while I stay at his house with Susan, drinking tea and talking. An hour or so after I've gone to bed I wake to him struggling with something in the room. I sit up, confused. He pushes a huge terra-cotta container with flowers toward the bed. It's at least two feet around, the kind of decorative pot one finds outside a store.

"Look," he says, laughing, clearly drunk. "I brought you flowers."

"Oh, my God." I cover my mouth, trying not to laugh. "You're crazy."

"Crazy about you," he says. He crawls into the bed with me, his hands still covered with dirt from the pot. He reeks of beer. He wraps his arms around my middle and kisses me. He slips off my T-shirt and underwear, and we make love. Really make love, which I've never done before him.

We kiss tenderly, look into each other's eyes. He moves slowly, waiting for me before he comes.

After, his breath even, his eyes closed, I tenderly brush a curl back from his face.

This is what it feels like to love a man.

Susan asks me to sit for her so she can paint me. I'm thrilled she thinks enough of me to want this. Each day, while Eli works, I sit for an hour in her studio while she paints.

When the painting is done, she gives it to me. The background is busy with flowered wallpaper. In contrast, my image is serene. I wear overalls, one strap falling off my shoulder, childlike. My expression is slightly sad. I try to see what she sees, who I really am.

Eli takes me out on a sailboat to his family's island. The sun sparkles on the bay. Little whitecaps scatter across the surface from the wind. The boat glides quickly. Eli shifts positions, keeping the sail taut while I sit back, admiring the scenery. Thick pines fill the many islands we pass. Osprey pass over the boat. Eli explains his mother's family is wealthy.

"My mom won't take any of the money," he says over the sound of the wind. "It's so stupid."

"She's mad at them," I say.

He looks over at me. I can see the anger in his eyes. "She can do whatever the fuck she wants, but she should consider me. I'd like that money. I'm fucking entitled to it."

I don't say anything, knowing whatever it is it will just piss him off further. I close my eyes, letting the wind blow my hair back, feeling the warm sun on my face.

"You don't know what it's like," he goes on. "You have money." He spits this last part.

"I'd take your mother over my family any day," I say, defensive.

"You can have her. The two of you can sit around and bitch about your families all day."

I press my lips together. He's being mean, and I'm starting to learn it's best to stay quiet when he's feeling that way.

Eli anchors the boat, and we take the small rowboat waiting at a buoy to the shore. An old, white clapboard house sits on the island. Gray driftwood is piled around the grassy meadow, and pine trees cluster behind the house. Inside, Eli explains the house has no electricity. Candle sconces line the walls for light in the evening. An old generator runs the plumbing.

We climb on to the large driftwood, no longer thinking about our argument on the boat, and make love outside in the sandy grass. We walk naked through the pinewoods surrounding the house, just because we can.

I don't ever want to leave.

The few times I do go back to New Jersey, I make Eli come with me. New Jersey is gray and busy. The highways are filled with cars, everyone heading somewhere in a hurry. I am continually edgy and twitchy here and afraid I'll run into one of the Rachels, but I never do. To combat the nervousness, I go shopping. It's old habit when I'm back here, the best way to stave off unwanted feelings. The first time I take Eli with me to the mall, though, I'm embarrassed. I don't want him to know this side of me, the side that wasted so many afternoons here, shopping for clothes with my father. For all the ways Eli feels gypped of the plush life he believes he's entitled to, he also has pride about his family's self-sufficiency. Perhaps because of what he didn't get, he's defensive about it. He gets mad when he sees things coming easily to other people. If he has to work hard, everyone else should too. So I'm surprised by the way his face lights up when, out of my guilt for being one of those people for whom things come easily, I offer to buy him clothes with my father's credit card. Eli eagerly leads me into Eddie Bauer and Banana Republic where we rack up Dad's bill.

To keep Eli with me, I also agree to quit smoking, and quitting winds up being much easier than I thought it would be.

In August, Dad and Nora rent another house in Dunewood on Fire Island, and we all take the ferry once again. The ocean stretches out beyond the deck of our house. The warm sun beats on to the sand. I see details I didn't notice last time I was here: the sparkling light on the water as the sun moves across the sky, tiny sand crabs that dig down into the sand when I try to catch them. Eli and I lie together on the deck with glasses of lemonade and work on our tans. Sometimes we hold hands. It's strange to be here again, this time with a boyfriend. I watch the teenagers lying on the beach, none of whom I recognize from two summers before. There's no sign of Justin, either, which is a relief. I don't have that old anxiety as I walk along the boardwalks, the terrible whisper at my ear: *Who will love me? Who will love me?* Eli loves me now.

About a week into our time on Fire Island, a longtime family friend, Bill, comes to stay for a few nights. He and his now ex-wife used to be close with Mom and Dad when they were married couples. They were one of the ones with a loft in SoHo. Like most of Mom and Dad's friends, Bill chose to remain friends with just one of them after the divorce. He chose Dad.

One night, sitting out on the deck and drinking too much wine, Bill tells me that following my parents' divorce, my mother tried to have custody of Tyler and me given to my grandparents. As he speaks, his voice full of outrage at my mother for trying to keep us from Dad, I suddenly remember myself at eleven, visiting a private high school somewhere near where my grandparents live in Florida. The memory comes to me as though from a great distance. I get nothing but the image – the large Spanish buildings, the spiky green grass – no feelings, no thoughts. I can smell the moist, earthy air, can sense the bright sun in my eyes, my sister and grandparents beside me. I think of those walks I know I took in New Jersey with Grandpa before my mother left. Did they even happen? Or were we actually in Florida, walking through a campus?

Later, Eli lies on the bed we share. He has a headache, having drunk too much. I know I should feel compassion. I should put a cold washcloth on his forehead, get him some water. But I'm too upset about Bill's comments, about being pulled back to that terrible time in my life. I want Eli to take care of me right now, not the other way around.

"You shouldn't have drunk so much," I tell him, frustrated.

"I'm aware of that," he mumbles.

"It's not like you've never drunk wine before. You should know your limit."

"How is your telling me this helping anything?" He groans and rolls over, away from me.

I lie on the bed next to him, feelings swarming in my chest.

"You never want to talk," I say.

He sighs, annoyed. "I have a headache," he says. "For God's sake, just leave me alone."

And that's when I start to cry. Part of me is crying for real, thinking about that difficult time in my past. But the other part of me hopes Eli will feel sorry for me. He'll turn over and put his arms around me, give me the kind of attention I crave.

He doesn't do that. He gets up, wincing as he does, and closes the door behind him. I lie there, the pain of his abandonment creeping through my body. I think of myself as that desperately sad girl in Florida, on the cusp of tremendous loss, walking among the grounds of a school she doesn't know. That lost girl grips my ribs, hooks her bones behind mine. She wants so much to be loved, to believe someone, anyone, will love her enough to stay. Will I ever be free of her?

As our sophomore year begins, Eli starts to get fed up with me. I drive too slowly and then too fast. I am too concerned about how I look, and then not enough.

I have started on a new birth control, suggested by my mother, and for the first week of each month, I throw up in the middle of the night. I also get one cold after another, and then a series of urinary tract infections. I'm in bed often, always recovering from one thing or another. Eli is unimpressed. He sees my illnesses as a sign of weakness, as more ways I'm too precious. I need to toughen up.

I don't doubt him. It's my first long relationship. I haven't learned yet that people bring their baggage along and then dump it over their partner's head. I figure he's found more about me that is unworthy, more that is not good enough. I try to be better.

Our sex takes a turn, as well, and not just because I am sick so much. Where at first I felt safe and free, I start to feel angry. Something happens when he touches my breasts in a certain way, or if he moves his hips just so. I don't like that he thinks he should get something from me, from my body. I want to push him off me and run. I can't stand the feel of him sometimes.

"What is the matter with you?" he asks again and again as I lie curled in the corner of the bed.

"I don't know."

He sighs angrily and stomps out of the room.

But it's true. I really don't know, and because I don't know, I start seeing a therapist.

Deirdre is in her mid-twenties, a graduate student interning for her master's degree. She has straight, mousy hair, blunt cut to her chin. Her features are round, her cheeks bright with rosacea. Even with so little experience, she has perfected the therapist gestures – the slightly cocked head, the gentle nods, pencil poised above her pad, like now as she waits for me to answer her question.

"Just angry," I tell her. "I don't know how else to describe it."

"Do you feel like you want to hurt him?"

I shake my head no. Sometimes I do, but I know this is too dangerous to say. She told me at the beginning of the session if she had reason to think I would hurt someone, she would have to breach our confidentiality.

She writes on her pad, then asks if someone in my past hurt me.

I shake my head.

"Force you to do something sexually you didn't want to do?" she asks.

The obvious question. Anyone who is raped or molested will have issues with being touched again. But I walked willingly into all my sexual experiences. And those times I didn't really want to, I didn't try to stop them. It could be said I even encouraged them. A slut in every way. I look down at my hands, which are gripped together, and shake my head again.

She asks about Eli and our fights.

"I just wish I didn't feel so needy all the time," I tell her.

"Tell me about your neediness."

I look out the small window, wondering where to begin. A squirrel rounds the trunk of a tree outside. Wind shakes the leaves, which are beginning to brown. After a moment, I start at the beginning. I tell her about Mom leaving and growing up in Dad's apartment. I tell her how my neediness feels ugly, a gaping red sore I don't want anyone to see.

"You don't like being vulnerable," she says.

I shake my head. I had never thought of it that way, but I suppose it's true. Being vulnerable makes me feel out of control, and when I'm out of control I'm unsafe, too aware anything can happen. I can be left. I can go unnoticed. I can be disregarded, like I'm not even there at all.

One weekend, visiting Maine, Susan pulls out a box

with baby photos of Eli. The three of us sit on the floor and exclaim over his adorable blond curls and pudgy body.

"I was so cute," Eli says.

"You really were." I put a hand on his knee.

"You were almost too cute," Susan says. "People would stop us on the street, commenting on it. You started to expect their attention."

"Nothing wrong with that," he says.

"We were spellbound by you too." Susan frowns, looking down. "We allowed you to get away with everything. We held you through your tantrums. We didn't give you any boundaries."

Eli rolls his eyes. "Here we go," he says to me. "Here comes the psychoanalyzing."

But I am intrigued. I want to know more.

"It's our fault you have so much anger," she says. She looks at him imploringly, wanting something, but Eli will have none of it.

Eli puts the photos he's holding back in the box. "Whatever, Mom," he says.

"Don't shut me out," Susan says, her voice a little hysterical. I look away, embarrassed for her. "Let's talk about this."

But Eli gets up and goes to his bedroom, and I follow him. "I hate it when she does that."

I sit beside him on the bed.

"I'm angry because I'm angry. Why does there have to be a reason for everything?"

"Maybe she's right, though," I say. "At least she's accepting blame."

He stands and starts yanking off his sweater. "I'm sick of her taking blame. I'm sick of her being such a fucking doormat with me."

I bite my lip.

Over the next few months, Eli and I fight more and more often about our sex life, which is dwindling down to almost nothing. He reminds me his ex-girlfriend loved sex. She experimented with lots of positions, wanted to do it in public and all the time. I try to explain this is unlike me. I used to want to have sex all the time too. I never used to feel so protective, like I don't want anyone touching me in that way. But this only makes him angrier.

By winter break, we decide to spend the vacation apart and see what happens. Eli lands a two-week-long internship in marine biology in Florida, and Mom wants Tyler and me to spend the holidays with her and her boyfriend, Donald, in the Berkshires, where my grandparents own a condominium. So after Eli and I say good-bye, I drive to join my family.

Mom takes us skiing and shopping at antiques stores and boutiques. We decorate a Christmas tree and wrap presents for each other. We're Jewish, but for reasons I never fully understood, Mom doesn't want to be, so we've always celebrated Christmas. Christmas morning, I unwrap a box from Mom that has two piles of cotton inside labeled with the words "right" and "left." She breaks into laughter.

"Get it?" she says, too loudly. "You said you wanted bigger boobs." She's referring to a few days before when, trying on a top, I commented on the fact my chest couldn't fill the spaces meant for breasts. I didn't mean I wanted big breasts, but as usual she's misconstrued the situation and used it to create attention for herself. She pulls Donald closer to look inside the box. "See? I labeled them left and right."

Donald laughs, accommodating her.

I give Tyler a look, needing an ally, but she smiles at Mom.

"Come on, Kerry," Mom says, seeing my expression. "Don't be so sensitive."

"I'm not being sensitive." I crumple the wrapping paper.

"Your breasts are fine just the way they are," she says.

When I say nothing, she pouts. "You have no sense of humor."

And when I still say nothing, she says, "You must hear about the outfit Claude is designing for me for my practice's grand opening. It's absolutely stunning. A black silk tunic and pajama pants. He's sewing in beads from a bracelet Grandma got in Indonesia."

Tyler nods. "I think you told us already. It sounds really nice."

I wish I never agreed to spend break this way.

Snow covers the ground and dark tree branches. Plows build piles taller than me along the side of the road, and because it keeps coming, Donald goes out in the morning to shovel the walkway to the car. Something about the snow, the quiet, the blankness, highlights my panic as I think about Eli. I decide I will do whatever it takes to keep him. I'll have sex more often. I'll stop needing so much from him. I know these thoughts are desperate, no different from the ones I had years ago with Heath, but I can't help it. Faced with losing Eli, I feel exactly as I did then, as though I haven't grown at all.

While Eli is in Florida, collecting specimens on a boat, I can't talk with him, which makes everything worse. Anxiety knocks against my ribs, keeping me awake at night. I wish I still smoked, just so I would have something to calm myself.

At dinner, Mom talks about her new practice, how Donald, who is a brain researcher, is now going for his MD as well. When I bring up studying Chaucer's *Canterbury Tales*, Mom gasps as though someone has grabbed her throat. I stop short.

"Did I mention yet the outfit Claude is designing for the grand opening?"

I set my mouth.

Tyler looks down.

"And the beads from Indonesia? The ones that Grandma

brought back?" She looks at Donald. "You saw the sketches. Isn't it beautiful?"

He nods. "It really is."

"I was talking here," I say.

"What?" Mom looks at me, innocent surprise on her face.

"I was talking about my Renaissance Literature class."

"Oh." She puts a jeweled hand to her throat, takes a sip of her wine. "I'm sorry. By all means, continue." Her expression changes to feigned interest.

"Forget it," I say.

"No," she says. "I want to hear."

"I don't care," I say, frustrated.

"OK, then," she says. She glances briefly at Donald for approval, and he smiles, a condescending smile that says I'm the one being immature.

"I'm going to bed," I say, though it's only seven thirty.

Mom frowns. "You need to learn to enjoy other people's company."

I don't say anything. Silence, I'm learning, is my only defense. I gather my plate and take it to the kitchen.

Later, Tyler comes downstairs to the room we share. I'm reading Hemingway's *Nick Adams Stories* for a class in school, his fictional exploration of coming of age. Each story recounts a traumatic event, and I'm struck by Nick's struggle to understand himself as a man in the face of each one. For all the times I've given myself over to them, all the energy I spend thinking about them, I still know nothing about men, about their hardships and hurts, the things that bring them to their knees. In my mind they're still invulnerable and too powerful. They still have all the control.

Tyler moves around the room, changing her clothes, looking for her own book. She is out of college now, and she lives in Chicago with her boyfriend. I want to ask her how she can stand it, being so far away, how she can trust he will keep loving her without being there to prove it, without his touch to know she truly exists. I don't know whether she's even thinking of him, if, like me, she can think of almost nothing else.

"Is it OK that this light is on?" I ask. I want to begin a conversation with her, but I don't know how to start.

"That's fine." She takes off her glasses, rests them beside the bed, and gets under the covers. She rolls over.

"It won't bother you?"

"Uh-uh."

I hesitate, place a bookmark on the page where I've stopped. "Tyler?"

"What is it?"

"Are you having any fun here?"

"I'm making the best of it."

"I don't want to be here."

She sighs, still facing away from me. "But you are, so why not just go with it?"

"I don't want to *just go with it*," I say, annoyed now.

She sighs again, annoyed too. "Are we done? I'm tired."

I set my mouth. "Fine."

I wait, my leg bouncing furiously on the bed, and soon her breath becomes long and even. I lean my head back and stare at the ceiling, too pissed now to sleep.

◆ ◆ ◆

THE DAY I know Eli is back in Maine, I call from a pay phone while Mom and Tyler are in the Price Chopper buying groceries. When he gets to the phone, he sounds different, distant.

"I miss you," I tell him. "I'll do whatever I need to make this work."

"Winter break isn't even over," he says. "Let's give it some time."

"I don't want to give it time," I say. "I just want you."

He doesn't say anything. I wait, my heart sick, knowing something has changed. People walk by behind me, scolding children, pushing rumbling carts full of disposable diapers and Diet Coke.

"Kerry," Eli starts.

"Oh, God."

"There was someone there, in Florida," he says.

"No."

"She goes to Clark," he says.

I squeeze my eyes shut, afraid I might throw up.

"Did you have sex with her?"

"No," he says. "We spent some time together. And we kissed."

I try to take a deep breath, but my lungs are too tight. I can't stand to think of it, of Eli and some nameless girl, his face close to hers.

"It's so easy with her. Relaxing."

"Don't," I say, stopping him. I want to cry. I can feel it lodged in my throat, but it won't come. The implication is clear: It's too hard with you. You're too hard. "Don't do this to us."

"It's already done," he says. "Before Florida it was already done."

"But I love you." For the first time I notice an elderly man is waiting for the phone. He stands back, respectful, seeing my face. He makes me feel even worse.

"I love you, too," Eli says. "I just don't think that matters enough anymore."

When we are done, I walk quickly along the sidewalk. Gray snow sits in piles against the curb. The air is icy. I hadn't noticed it while on the phone, but now it begins to seep into my skin. I like it, this physical sensation. It distracts me from the dull ache I feel. I stand at the entrance to Price Chopper. I cannot go inside. An old lady pushes her cart. A woman walks by with a little boy who jumps and jumps. It is all too ordinary. Too sharply different from the chaos I feel inside. So I wait for Mom and Tyler in the cold.

◆ ◆ ◆

BACK AT SCHOOL, I waste no time. Shawn thinks I'm cute, so I start with him. Then Alex. Then Greg. One of them, I can't remember which, tells me I'm a femme fatale because I suck men in and then spit them out. He has no idea.

Eli takes up with the girl he met in Florida. The first time I see her, I want to slit my throat – or hers. She is beautiful, with porcelain skin and straight black hair. She's the picture of old money, right out of a J. Crew catalog. She's what I imagine the estranged part of Eli's family looks like, the part that owns that island. I do my best to avoid anywhere I know Eli might be, but there are times I'm blindsided. When I catch glimpses of them together I feel physical pain, like someone has punched me in the gut. I take up smoking again, and more and more boys.

Nights I'm alone, I lie in bed, aching, hating my need, my big, nasty need, the thing that makes me unlovable.

◆ ◆ ◆

A WEEKEND AT home. I sit around the apartment, not wanting to do anything. Dad offers to take me shopping, but even that sounds depressing to me. Nora makes me egg breakfasts with good bagels from the local deli. She sits with me while I read a book.

"Honestly?" she says. "He was too handsome."

"This isn't helping," I tell her.

"I mean it." She sets down her book and her red wire-rimmed glasses. "Miranda's father was very handsome. So was the man I dated just after him. But they were also schmucks. Good-looking men think they can have whatever they want. They get coddled too much."

I pull my legs up beneath me. "But I'm attracted to them."

"We all are, honey. But take it from me. I stopped dating very handsome men a long time ago."

"Hey," Dad says as he comes out of his bedroom. "I heard that."

Nora just smiles. "Don't take it too personally, love," she tells him.

Spring vacation, I get Dad to take me skiing in Taos, New Mexico. I have wanted for a long time to see the Southwest – the muted colors, the long, sloping mountains, landscape celebrated in the books and films by and about Native Americans I read and see in my classes. As we drive in our rental car from Albuquerque, I am not disappointed. The mountains are like sculpture, the sky an ashen blue. This is exactly what I need.

Chances are, my dad needs this too. Just a few months ago he lost his job as vice president of engineering at the company where he had been for thirteen years. Some kind of management takeover. He got a hefty severance, and as an innovative designer, he won't have trouble finding a new job. But he's quick to anger, and he also seems depressed. He was a head honcho in his last job, worked up to be vice president and had been offered the presidency many times. He had designed the company's star products, and his staff admired and deferred to him. He had attained celebrity status in the world of water heating design. Years later, someone in the field will say to me, "That's your father? That man is your *father*? Will you introduce me?" as though I just told him my father was Robert DeNiro. He was also losing a salary that had grown to tremendous proportions over the years. Now he has to establish that somewhere else. At his age, he tells me, he shouldn't have to reestablish himself in his career. Even though he'll be footing the bill, taking this trip together is my way of trying to help him feel better, just like those shopping trips used to do for me.

The day after we arrive in Taos, the Gulf War begins. We watch on the wide-screen television in the bar with the other resort guests as the United States bombs Iraq. We sip our drinks, wide-eyed for four days. And then it is done.

At dinner, eating dirty rice and ceviche, we discuss the war, its distance, its irrelevance to our lives. A child of the Cold War, I didn't think I would experience real war in my lifetime, and if I did, I thought it would be monumental. This feels like a movie I just happened to catch on TV. Dad talks about the media and the ways in which what we saw about the war is shaped to make us feel good. "We don't know what really happened," he warns.

One night, a guy catches my eye. He smiles at me from the bar where he sits alone. On my way back from the bathroom, he touches my arm and invites me to join him. He has a strong accent, from France it turns out. He has been visiting for the past week, and his friends have gone home already. Tonight is his final night.

Two hours later, François and I are naked in his room. We have sex three times before dawn, when he leaves in a taxi and I climb into the sleeping loft in Dad's and my room and sleep for most of the day. Dad asks no questions, as usual.

The next night, I meet Amos. Amos works at the resort, so he takes me to the staff's private hot tub where I give him a blow job before we fuck.

To my delight, I haven't thought of Eli more than once the whole trip.

Nine

THERE IS A new boy I like. I see him every other day when our classes let out at the same time. He has long, dark hair and unbelievably beautiful eyes. He sits on the campus lawn with a few other guys and passes around a joint. My friends, who I see more of now that Eli is out of the picture, tell me about him. His name is Leif, a music major. He plays guitar in a band, and they are pretty sure he doesn't have a girlfriend. They walk over there with me, and almost immediately I can feel the energy between us, the promise of something to come.

The night of my upstairs neighbor's party, a party where I know Leif will be, I lie in my bed with my friend Bevin plotting seduction. I will use pot I took from my dad ages ago and haven't smoked, and I'll dress as hot as possible. We giggle, excited for me, excited for what might happen tonight.

When Leif walks into the party, I keep him on my radar, waiting for the right moment. And when he is alone a moment, filling his beer from the keg in the kitchen, I pounce. He follows me downstairs to my apartment to get high, and I take out a bowl and the bag of pot and hand it to him. We sit on my bed and he lights up and passes it to me. We chat about our classes, where we're from. Even in the haze of getting high, I can't feel calm. All I want is for him to kiss me, to put his hands on me. There is something about him, his scent, the way he looks. I don't know. My desire for him is fierce. I could tear his clothes off. I could eat him off a plate.

At each awkward silence, I wait, poised for that kiss.

"Listen," he says finally, "I'm very attracted to you."

I smile.

"But there's a situation you should know about."

My smile drops.

He explains he's been seeing someone. He doesn't think he wants to stay with her, but she's his friend, and he should probably break up with her before anything else happens. I nod, trying to look calm. Inside, my heart is filling. He wants me more than this girl.

"Whatever you need to do," I say. But as I do, I turn my body toward him, opening myself.

He nods, his eyes on mine.

And then he kisses me. We move quickly, removing each other's clothes. He moves over me, then in me. Our sex is crazed, animal-like. And it doesn't stop there. We have sex four more times before we finally fall asleep at dawn. Even asleep, though, we're aroused, and we wake again and again for more.

At nine the next evening, we agree we should probably get some food. We joke about feeding other needs. We take a shower together, and then drive to a nearby Thai restaurant. The other customers politely chat, their napkins on their laps. They dip their chopsticks gracefully into their food. We, on the other hand, should be ripping raw flesh with our teeth, blood dripping down our chins. Or at least that's how it feels after all the sex. We glance at each other shyly, trying to come up with things to say. There's no way to get around the weirdness. Sure we shared bodily fluids, our most intimate places. But we've barely exchanged anything else.

When we get back, it's close to one in the morning. Leif leaves to head back to his apartment. He's explained that the girl he's been seeing lives in the apartment above his with a group of three other girls, and they'll all know he didn't come home last night. It's like a coven up there, he says. The four of them may as well be stirring a brew. But he has to face the consequences eventually.

I watch him go and then climb into bed. The sheets smell like him. We didn't establish anything about whether we'd see each other again. I stare up at the ceiling, unable to sleep, a tangle of desire inside.

Three days pass, and I hear nothing. At night I can barely sleep; every sound is him. Twice I get up, pad into the kitchen, and open the door, sure I will see him there. But it's just my roommates, or the wind, or strangers passing by. I tell Bevin I've never been with anyone so incredibly good-looking. He's probably too good-looking for me. But she just frowns. "He's not too good for you," she says. "Why would you say that?"

Then, on the fourth day, while cleaning, something great happens: I find a folded piece of paper under my bed. I open it to find lines of music notes scribbled across the page. Leif.

From the student center pay phone, my heart bursting, I call him, and when he comes to the phone, I tell him about the paper. I don't describe it, afraid he'll determine it's something he doesn't need. I tell him it looks important, and he agrees to come by that evening to pick it up.

When he arrives, I'm ready. I've been ready for an hour. For days. Since the second he left me that night and I watched him lope away. My hair is perfect. I'm wearing an outfit that is both sexy and looks like I threw it on without a thought – well-worn jeans and an old T-shirt that hangs off one shoulder and reveals a glimpse of my stomach when I lift my arms. I lead him to my bedroom and hand him the piece of paper. He looks at it, but only for a moment. I see he's not here for the paper. My throat is tight with anticipation.

"She was really upset," he says. He sits on my bed. I sit beside him. I can smell him, his scent, warm and spicy.

I nod my head, trying to look sympathetic. What I want to know is, *Are you mine now?*

"It's been pretty bad, actually." He leans his elbows on his knees. He runs his fingers across the fold of the paper. I am hyperaware of him, of his hands, his legs.

"What are you going to do?" I ask.

"I don't know." He glances at me. "I think I should just stay away."

Stay away. My throat tightens. Stay away from me?

"There were so many times this past week I almost came back here."

He looks right at me now.

"Really?" I'm overwhelmed, just knowing he was thinking of me. I'm so used to my fantasies being, well, fantasies. And here, he may well have been standing at my door like I had hoped. "Why didn't you?"

He shakes his head. "I wanted to, believe me. It's been bad at my place. I've been in hell every day, afraid of what she'll do. Her roommates trap me when I get home and try to talk me into staying with her." His brow is creased. He's clearly stressed. "Do you have any more of that weed?"

I take it out, watch as he lights a bowl. He holds it out to me, but I shake my head. I can't help but think of Eli and that girl, how he had said being with her was easy compared to being with me. I don't like to think of Leif's ex-girlfriend, feeling the kind of pain I felt with Eli, but I push that from my mind. Leif lights it a few more times, sucking hard until it's all but cashed. As he blows out smoke, he seems to relax a bit.

"You could just stay here," I try. "Until things blow over."

He nods, shakes the bowl a little, and holds it up to the light. "Do you have a paper clip or something?"

I find him a paper clip from my desk, and he rubs it in the bowl, separating the charred bits. Then he lights it again.

"It wouldn't be a problem," I say. "I could leave the front door open for you at night."

I watch him, hopeful.

He nods again. "That might not be a bad idea." He puts down the bowl and turns to me. The crease in his forehead is gone. His gaze is loose, his eyes red. And we start to kiss.

We stay in bed again through the next afternoon.

Our conversations are brief and pointed, the kind of conversations people only have when in bed together.

"You have beautiful eyes," I tell him.

"No, *you* have beautiful eyes. And this part of you," he says, running his hand along my hip. "I love this."

He leaves to go to class, but this time he's coming back that night.

I go to class too, feeling sexy, light, a girl others might want to be.

Once, in the student center, I see the girl Leif left for

me. Her eyes make little slits as we pass, but rather than guilt or fear, I feel elated. He chose me over her.

Leif and I have tons of sex, standing against walls, in locked bathrooms at parties, on the floor of my bedroom. We can't keep our hands off each other. During the day, we part to go to our separate classes. I listen to lectures on *The Faerie Queene,* discuss symbolism in *The Glass Menagerie,* all the while aware of Leif's scent still on my skin. At two or three in the morning every night, Leif comes into my apartment after working on music compositions in the studio, and he finds me in bed, waiting for him. Because I know he will come, the waiting is delicious, so different from what waiting has been in the past. My body is always aroused, just waiting.

On Spree Day, a campus tradition when classes are canceled and all the students party, Leif and I go back to my room to have sex. Outside, I hear students yelling and laughing. Music streams from someone's radio. Lots of kids take acid on Spree Day. Or they carry jugs of vodka and orange juice. They smoke joints right out in the open on the green. You can always tell which ones are tripping by their huge pupils. They look past you like you're not even there. Leif strips off my clothes and then his. He presses his mouth to my neck. I close my eyes, all my senses alive. I can't imagine being happier, more filled.

Sometimes I see Eli around campus. He is still with that girl, but it's different now that I have Leif; it's that easy to replace the spot Eli took up in my heart. He was my first real love, but I can speak of him as someone in my past. Leif is with me now. He plays gigs at parties around campus and in the Pub. We arrive together to parties, and guys shake his hand, ask him about his playing. They nod at me, his girlfriend. While he plays guitar, girls dance. They look up at him with desire, and it gives me great pleasure to walk up to him during his breaks and kiss him, knowing they're watching.

◆ ◆ ◆

A COUPLE MONTHS after we start seeing each other, I go to the bathroom while at a party, and I'm horrified to see something small and crablike crawl up from my pelvis. I brush it off me. I'd been itchy down there, I realize now, but I hadn't thought much about it. Freaked, I set out to find Leif.

Sure enough, we both have crabs. He tells me his ex had them when they first started sleeping together, but he thought they were gone. She got her revenge, I suppose.

We use his leftover crab shampoo that night and wash our sheets, and he finds some poison that works to kill them in the carpet and couch.

Just a few weeks later, though, I notice something else strange down there, little tags of pale skin. My heart pounding, I call my mother.

"Oh, Kerry," she says when I describe it.

"What?" I ask, flipping out. "What is it?"

"I can't diagnose without seeing it," she says, "but it sounds like HPV."

My heart stops. Three letters, just one away from a deadly disease.

"What's that?"

She explains human papillomavirus to me. Genital warts. She talks about rates of infection and populations seeing the biggest increases while I grip the phone, feeling sick. When it comes to medicine, she's always interested in telling me everything she knows. She doesn't listen for what I really need right now, which is reassurance. Being a doctor, and the prestige that comes with it, is so immensely important to her, so much more important than being a mom. That's not new information. She left Tyler and me to become a doctor. But her preference can still sting.

In the morning, Leif and I go together to the Planned Parenthood, where they take us into separate examination rooms. My nurse is tall and no-nonsense. She pulls the hot light down so it showcases my vagina and pushes at the folds of skin down there with her fingers. Then she slides in a speculum.

"Did you have sex recently?" she asks.

I nod. Of course I have.

"You shouldn't have before you came here," she says, her voice tight.

"Not since last night," I tell her defensively. "And I took a shower this morning."

She sighs, annoyed. "There's still semen in here, making it difficult for me to determine what's your fluid and what's someone else's."

I press my lips tightly together, ashamed. I can't even determine who gave me the warts. According to my mother, incubation for HPV is three months, so it could have been François or Amos in New Mexico. Or it could have been one of the guys I slept with before Taos. I don't need anyone to tell me how bad that is, I can't even isolate where I got them. I don't need anyone else to tell me what a slut I really am.

"I'm sorry," I say.

"Well," she says, "we'll just have to do our best."

She does a Pap smear and then takes a small bottle out of a cabinet. She explains she'll need to use some type of acid to burn off the warts, and I'll need to come back for a few more treatments until they are gone. She also explains the Pap will reveal whether I'm in danger of cervical cancer, which some forms of HPV threaten to cause.

I close my eyes, scared, as she applies something to my labia. The acid stings like crazy, but I hold myself still, not wanting to further disappoint the nurse. When I sit up, she looks me in the eye. Her face is stern. "You shouldn't have sex again until these are gone. Otherwise you risk infecting your partner."

I lower my eyes, sick with shame.

I find Leif waiting for me, and we go out to my car.

He's happy because he didn't get infected, and I'm relieved. If he had, I would have felt even worse than I already do. I lower myself slowly into the driver's seat like an old person, my rear still sore. But I don't complain. I got what I deserve.

Mom calls later that day.

"How are you doing?" she asks. "I've been thinking about you. I know today's the day you went to the clinic."

"I'm OK." I lie in bed, cradling the phone with my head. She can be caring like this sometimes, like the mother I've always wanted her to be. I think of what Eli's mother told me about the Alzheimer's releasing her mother's more loving self. It helps me to know there is this part to my mother. There is a possibility that somewhere inside, if it weren't for all her own hurts and insecurities, she might really love me. I close my eyes, wishing as I do at times she were here with me, smoothing my hair.

"Be sure to take care of yourself," she says. "Is Leif there? Is someone tending to you?"

"I'm really OK," I say again. "Leif is in his studio, getting a composition done before class. But I'm fine. Only a little sore."

"All right. Don't stay there all alone. Call a friend."

"I will."

We hang up and I force myself to rise. I turn on the CD player, which plays a Tom Waits song. I think about going somewhere. A coffee shop. The student center. Calling

Bevin, maybe, like Mom said. But ultimately I just get back into bed. Some days nothing sounds good.

◆ ◆ ◆

WHEN SUMMER COMES, Leif goes home to New Hampshire to perform with his band, and I stay in my apartment at school. I have nowhere else to go, no friends left in New Jersey, no internship or job like some of my friends. I've allowed Eli, and then Leif, to occupy my entire life, enough that I have not begun to focus on anything meaningful in my life. In high school, Rachel A once told me she aspired to be a housewife. She wanted to live the cliché, watching soap operas and eating all day. She didn't want to have to perform out in the world. But I don't feel like that. I love vibrant discussions about literature. I love to write. I sit in the front row of most classes with my hand raised. There are things I know I'm good at, if I'd only keep my focus there.

Seeing this discrepancy in my life begins to nag at me, like a child tugging on my sleeve. What am I doing? Why can't I ever just focus on me? My therapist and I discuss this, and she encourages me to create something in my life that will hold my interest. So I apply for an August writing workshop and am accepted.

As often as possible, I drive up to Leif's to see him. His family lives in a big, sterile house in the country. The front yard is a long, lovely stretch of wildflowers, and at the end of the driveway, behind the house, woods encase a pristine lawn. Leif is so perfect to me, so surreal, it is hard for me to grasp the idea of him growing up here, with parents, in a small town, like any other kid.

Leif's father is friendly, also a musician. He works with computers, but in his spare time he sits with Leif and they work out phrases or play jazz. He watches Leif play with admiration and pride, and he admits he wishes he could play music rather than work in his field. Leif's mother is different. She admires Leif's talent and drive like his father, but she holds herself at a distance, cold and detached. I try to engage her in conversations, but she rarely wants to talk. We don't think the same, like Susan and I did. I can tell she thinks I'm flighty with my interest in psychology. Or, who knows, maybe she's worried I'm analyzing her. Either way, I can feel her disapproval of me. She thinks I'm not good enough for her son.

As soon as we are out of his parents' house, Leif gets high. We meet his bandmates, he smokes some more with them, and I watch them rehearse or play gigs in town. We regularly get back to his house in the early morning hours, and then Leif sleeps until two or three the next day. He keeps his room dark to ward off daylight, and when I stay there I find I'm always groggy and often bored. I wake long before him and sneak down to the kitchen to find something to eat, thankful his parents are at work. When I grow bored enough, I crawl back into bed and nudge him to have sex, just for something to do.

When he does wake, he moves slowly. He gets himself something to eat, goes to the piano room, and plays with a composition he's been working on. I follow him from room to room.

"Let's do something," I say, sitting on the piano bench next to him.

"Like what?" He leans forward and erases a note, writes a new one in. His handwriting is chicken scratch, but his musical notes are always neat and perfectly shaped.

"I don't know," I say. "Anything. Let's go out for lunch."

"Isn't it too late for lunch?" He begins to play again. He really is very good.

"Then dinner."

He grimaces. "I just got up. I don't really want to go anywhere."

I sigh, resigning myself. After a few more minutes of sitting I walk around the house, looking at art and photos on the wall. There is a traditional painting of a man on a horse, another of a bouquet of roses. I think about how different Leif is from this art, which is safe and straightforward, nothing beneath the surface. Leif is intensely creative. His music takes risks. I wonder how he fits in amid this family, if he shoulders the burden of being the family risk-taker, so they don't have to. I can't help but notice how he acts around them, always happy and even, but then as soon as he's away he gets high or he sleeps.

I also don't find any pictures of Leif as a child. When I ask him, he goes into his closet and takes down a shoebox of photos.

"I was fat as a kid," he explains as I sift through the pictures of Leif and his friends. It's true he was chubby, but he wasn't so big as to be called fat.

"There are no baby pictures?" I ask.

He shrugs. "I suppose there are somewhere."

I examine each picture, wanting more. "How could your parents have no baby pictures of you?"

He shrugs again, and I notice I'm annoyed. Annoyed he doesn't demand more from his parents. Annoyed by the hazy film that seems to cover everything in this house, including him.

I nod and put the photos back in the box, not wanting him to see my frustration. I wrap my arms around his neck and pull him to me. He hugs back, which makes me feel better. Connected to him again.

◆ ◆ ◆

AFTER THE HPV scare, a small panic remains in my stomach. What if there's something more going on? What if I have HIV? Most of my friends have gotten tested. It's the reasonable thing to do if you've had sex with more than one person, especially unprotected sex, of which I've had lots.

One friend even gets tested every six months as a precaution. I nod along with them, but I'm a terrible hypocrite. I've slept with many more strangers than they have, and I've yet to get tested. I'm too scared. In the eighties, AIDS plagued gay men, IV drug users, and people receiving blood transfusions. It felt unrelated to me. Now HIV is showing up in the blood of more and more heterosexual women. We're getting it at the fastest rate in the country.

On a Monday morning, I drive back to the same Planned Parenthood. I tell the receptionist why I'm there, and a young woman takes me into the back. As we walk, my heart beats so fast I feel like I might pass out. This woman is kinder than the last one. She's young, not much older than me. Perhaps it's more acceptable to get a voluntary test than to show up with an STD. She puts a warm hand on my arm as she guides me into a small, white room that has only a desk and two chairs. She sits across from me and sets a clipboard on the desk.

"I need to ask you some questions before we take your blood," she tells me.

"Questions?" My voice quakes.

"These are standard questions we ask everyone. It's mandatory counseling before the test."

I bite my lip. "OK."

She looks down at the paper. "Are you currently sexually active?"

I nod.

She makes a mark. "Do you currently have more than one sexual partner?"

"No."

"In your sexual history, have you had more than five partners?"

"Um, yeah."

"More than ten?"

I bite my lip again. "Yes."

She doesn't look at me, just marks her paper.

"In your sexual history, was there ever a time when you had more than one sexual partner in the span of a month?"

I take a breath, let it out slowly. "Yes."

"Are you currently using birth control?"

"The Pill," I say.

"Good." She writes that. "What about condoms?"

I shake my head. What must she be thinking of me?

"In your sexual history, did you consistently use condoms?"

I shake my head again.

She makes a few more marks. "OK," she says. "I need to advise you to use condoms every time you engage in intercourse. It's the only effective way to protect yourself from disease."

"I know that," I say. I want to tell her I'm not stupid. I know everything there is to know about protecting myself. I'm well aware of how HIV and STDs are transmitted. But I also know my behavior defies my knowledge.

"Listen," she says, perhaps hearing my defensiveness. "You're not the only one who comes through these doors and tells me about multiple partners without condoms."

I smile slightly. "I'm not?"

"God, no." She smiles too. "It's frustrating, though. I mean, if you know to use condoms, why don't you?"

She stares at me. She's not being condescending. This is an honest question. There are many more like me, and she wants to understand.

I shake my head. "I'm not sure," I say.

After, another woman draws my blood and tells me to set an appointment for fourteen days from then – fourteen long days – to get my results. Driving home, I think about the first woman's question, wishing I had said more. I do know why I haven't used condoms when I should have. In the moment, when I'm busy trying to make some guy mine, thoughts about death or disease are furthest from my mind. I'm too caught up in desperation, in filling what I can never seem to fill. It's a terrible realization that I'm willing to risk my life to get to that place.

I visit Leif in those fourteen days, trying to keep my mind off it. He brushes me off, tells me my anxiety is irrational. But he doesn't know the truth about my past, those two random guys in Taos, all those nameless guys before them. When the day comes, I'm a wreck. I didn't sleep much the night before. Then I drank too much coffee to compensate. I stand in the waiting room, too jumpy to sit.

I feel like I might throw up. That same woman, the one with all the questions, comes to get me, and as we walk down the hallway I try to interpret the look on her face. Is she about to tell me I'm going to die? She opens the door to the same stark room and sets a folder in front of her as she sits. I'm going to throw up right here, in this tiny white room.

"Your test was negative," she says.

"Oh, my God!" I say, relief flooding me. Then, "You really shouldn't act so stoic on the way in here. You might send someone into cardiac arrest."

She smiles. "I'll work on that."

"So I can go?"

"Just use condoms," she says. "OK?"

I smile. I think about telling her what I came to in the car, the answer to her question last time. But I just want to get out of here now. Out of this ridiculously small room and back into the world.

"I will," I say.

And then I do what everyone must do in this situation. I tell myself I will do things differently from now on. If Leif and I should split, I'll use condoms. I'm nobody's fool.

◆ ◆ ◆

IN AUGUST, I drive to Vermont for my month-long writing workshop, and all the anxiety I avoided by not doing something like this, all my fear about leaving the world of boys, fills me. I'm not nervous about my writing or being somewhere new. I'm nervous about being away from Leif. Out of his sight, I'm afraid I don't matter. I hate admitting it. I still experience myself like I did in high school. Without a man loving me, I feel like I don't exist.

He has promised to visit me for the third weekend, and I've already begun to count down the days.

The Vermont campus is beautiful. Purple and yellow irises cluster near huge, heavy oaks. Maple trees wave leaves as big as my hand. Mountains hover in the distance. After I settle into my single room, I go for a run, a new activity I have taken up under Deirdre's advice. I run along gravel roads, thick greenery on either side. The sky is a piercing blue, the air hot. When I return I feel enlivened, sharp. I can do this, I think.

That first evening I meet the other workshop partici-pants at a welcome dinner. There are only a few of us who are young, so we gravitate toward one another. One girl, Kelly, slinks toward me and whispers, "Where are all the hot men?"

I laugh. "All the hot men are painters and musicians. Writers aren't hot."

She smiles. "Speak for yourself."

Kelly is a few years older than me, though she seems even older. She scans the room, her eyes dark. She wears red lipstick that extends just beyond the lines of her lips, and she holds her lips in a well-rehearsed pout. Maybe she doesn't realize how obvious this is, how it looks like she's trying too hard. I don't know her at all, but I feel both sad and scared for her, seeing those lips.

Before the dinner is through, two older men approach her. She opens her body toward them, and when they speak she lowers her head and widens her eyes. Another practiced move. I squirm inside, aware I have my own moves: big smile, wide eyes, cocked head.

Days, I work on my first short story. It is about a girl who is struck mute in an accident. In my critique, the teacher tells me the character remains undeveloped. Her muteness doesn't go anywhere. It stays static, which makes the whole story incomplete.

I work on it some more.

In between I go running, allowing the fresh, flowery air to clear my head.

I think about Leif. Only seven days to go.

I call him twice from the pay phone in the dormitory lobby. The first time he's not home, and I leave a message with his mother. The second time, he sounds groggy, like he just woke up. We talk briefly about the workshop and his gigs, and then he has to go.

"I miss you so much," I tell him.

"I miss you, too."

I want to make him promise, but I hold myself back.

"I'll see you in just five days."

225

"That's right."

"You're still coming, right?"

"I just said I was."

"OK," I say, not wanting to let him go.

"Right. I'll see you then."

And he hangs up.

I find Kelly and a few others lying on a blanket in the grass, and I join them. They're discussing the writing life, submissions and rejections, magazines with which they've placed work.

"What about you?" one of the girls asks. "Do you send your stuff out?"

"I just started writing," I say. "I'm not ready."

"That's good," Kelly says. She stretches out her legs in the sun. She has less makeup on today, and you can see how pretty she really is, freed up from all that pretense and effort. "You should wait. Too many people send out their stuff before it's ready."

"That's right," the other girl says. "Too many are focused on publication, not the writing. But if you rush the process, the writing isn't good. You lose the whole purpose of having written."

"That's one of the things I love about writing," Kelly says now. Her eyes are lit up. "I love the surprise. You never know where it will take you."

I listen, rapt, excited. *This*. I want this. The first thing, other than boys, that feels meaningful to me, that I can feel in my veins, can literally feel moving its way through me like a drug.

I go back to my room to work on my story some more.

◆ ◆ ◆

THE DAY LEIF arrives, I'm ecstatic. I can't wait to get my arms around him, to get him near me. I pace my room, making myself wait to take my shower and get ready. It would be unbearable to be dressed too early. I try to read, but I can't keep the sentences in my head.

As soon as he arrives, we strip down and have sex. Then we go out for some food. He comes with me to a poetry reading that evening, but he fidgets beside me. I know he has no interest in any of this. So after the reading, when I would normally socialize with the other participants at the reception, discussing the reading and our own writing, I go back to my room with Leif. He takes out his guitar and noodles around on it for a while. I lie on my bed and watch him, then take out a book and try to read. But that restlessness moves right in again as though it arrived with him, a package deal.

When he leaves, I am just a tiny bit relieved.

Kelly, who has been hesitant to workshop her story, brings in copies during the final week. Having finished my rewrite, I too hand out my story. Kelly's is about a girl whose father gives weekly ear cleanings. The writing is suggestive and harrowing, and it's clear something terrible and lascivious happens during these ear cleanings. We all rave, impressed. By now, Kelly is the talk of the workshop, but not for her writing. The way she walks, her pout. All the men whisper comments to each other. The girls keep their distance. I feel sad for her. She overwhelms her talent with this need for attention. Her talent isn't enough.

The second to last night of the workshop, Kelly shows up to the reading wearing a tight minidress patterned with big red cherries. We all watch as she approaches, flirts with, and then leaves with the author who read. Before reading her story, I didn't see our connection. Now I get how much we're alike. She is me in bold print. I can't know for sure whether her story is autobiographical, but it gets me thinking about my own past, about the lack of boundaries in my family. Is this why I've handed over my body to so many boys?

The next day, the teacher reads my story aloud. Listening to her read, I'm amazed I wrote it. It's actually good. She congratulates me for progressing so much in the short time we've been together.

"You're a real writer," she says.

Her words feel like salvation.

◆ ◆ ◆

SENIOR YEAR. I turn myself toward writing. I find a fiction tutor since my college doesn't have a creative writing department, and I start pumping out stories. As Dad warned, truths begin to slip out now that the war is long over. The long-standing fires in Kuwait, our country's backing out of supporting the Shiites. Angry, I join other students to march and rally for peace in the Middle East. I take on an editor position for Clark's alternative, liberal newspaper. I don't know as much as I should, but it feels good to get behind something, to channel my anger into something real.

Leif moves into an apartment with a mutual friend and her boyfriend, and I find an apartment by myself. I try not to focus on the fact that the girl Leif lives with is stunningly beautiful. I don't want to be one of those jealous girlfriends who doesn't let her man have friendships with other girls, beautiful or not. But almost immediately, it starts to get to me. What I really hoped was he would want to live with me. Instead, he opted to live with the prettiest girl on campus.

"What about with the bathroom?" I ask him when I come to see his new place. "Does she come out of there in a towel?"

"I don't know, Kerry," he says. "I haven't noticed."

"Yeah, right."

"I'm living with her and her boyfriend."

I sit on his bed. I want something more from him, I'm just not sure what. To tell me I'm prettier? That he loves me only? That he'll never love anyone else? I'm being stupid, I know, especially since I'm finding myself more and more bored with him. Our interests are too disparate. But this truth nags at me, making me cling tighter.

"Kerry," he says, seeing the way I look, "this is ridiculous."

"She's very insecure," I tell him. I wince inside. This girl I'm talking about is my friend. This is my friend whom I'm degrading.

"I don't like her," he says. "Can we drop it?"

I press my lips together, knowing he's right.

◆ ◆ ◆

TYLER'S GETTING MARRIED. Our father, in typical I-won't-hear-it-if-it-makes-me-uncomfortable style for which we all make fun of him, calls me a month before her wedding.

"Tyler's getting married," he says with shock in his voice.

"I know, Dad. You do too," I tell him. "We've all known for almost a year."

But I can relate. It really is hard to believe. She's made a point of being anti-marriage for a long time. A few years ago, when I told her I wanted to get married someday, even though our parents divorced, she said she didn't.

"Mom and Dad never should have gotten married either," she told me. "They were too different. Not at first, of course. But they went in different directions, like most people do over time. Humans aren't supposed to mate for life. Patriarchal religions made that up so women would be under men's control. Marriage is bullshit."

But handmade invitations with sketches of herself and her fiancé, Gill, that say, "We're getting hitched!" arrive in the mail.

Leif and I fly to Chicago for the wedding, which is really just a small party at a local bar she and her fiancé frequent. My mother is there with her boyfriend. Dad and Nora are there too. My sister wears yellow cowboy boots and a black dress that shows off the many illustrative tattoos on her back. Gill is in a charcoal gray jacket with a turquoise bolo. They stand at the back of the bar in front of a painting of Spike Lee and thank everyone for coming to celebrate their union. Tyler looks happy, but also something else. Sheepish, embarrassed. I'm not sure what. I hug her and say I'm happy for her, but really I'm bugged. Maybe it's because she's doing this thing she was so clearly against. Maybe it's because she doesn't seem to be taking it seriously. Whatever it is, I feel angry with her, and also worried.

When I tell Leif later, he shrugs and suggests I let it go. But I can't. It's all too familiar, her need for this security. She keeps it hidden behind her tough, anticorporate façade. She talks loudly about all the ways she's getting screwed, about the environment, the government, everything but her real self. I know what that feels like, that kind of vulnerability. I know how scary it is to have it hang out there, how much I work to hide it too. In truth, I would marry Leif in a second. I would marry almost anyone in a second, if that would make me feel loved.

◆ ◆ ◆

JUST A FEW months later, Leif's and my beautiful friend and her boyfriend break up, and Leif is left with no housing. I suggest he live with me, and though he is still hesitant, he agrees under one condition: We'll keep separate rooms, like proper roommates. I hate that he wants this. He doesn't want our lives to meld. But I am well practiced at taking what I can get.

The fact that his marijuana dealer just moved in one floor below me can't hurt my cause either.

He takes the room I had set up as my office, but after a few weeks I work myself into that room too, and it becomes our shared bedroom.

With Leif firmly in my grasp, I focus more and more on writing. I apply to MFA programs, my top choice in Arizona. Leif applies to music programs, including the same school in Arizona.

On Spree Day, we lie in bed, listening to the excitement and music outside the window. Leif reaches for me, and we make love. But unlike last year, I feel restless. I lie beneath him, uninterested, wishing he'd hurry up. I want to get outside, into the world. I want to feel like I did last year, enlivened and full.

I build a schedule. Every morning I wake at six a.m. On alternate mornings I write for three hours before my first class, and on the other days I run three miles around the indoor track at the gym. During the day I attend class, work at the local bookstore, and am back in bed by ten. Leif has a schedule too. He sleeps until noon, then goes to his studio until two or three in the morning, leaving only for classes or to grab a snack.

I like my days. I like that I feel productive and energized.

Many nights, though, I wake when Leif comes home. I haven't seen him all day. I watch him disappear into the bathroom and lie awake, listening. We haven't had sex in weeks, living on different timetables. Moon shadows shroud the room. A car hisses by outside. I listen hard, thinking maybe I hear him masturbating. Years ago I used to do the same thing with my father, lying on the futon in his living room, thinking I heard him and his girlfriend having sex. Like those times, I feel slightly turned on, a voyeur to something I shouldn't know, but I also feel terribly alone.

When he comes to bed, I shift, wanting him to know I'm awake. I hold myself still, hoping he'll move toward me, hoping we'll make love, hold each other, anything.

But he turns away from me, asleep.

If things weren't heading south enough, Dad calls to say he and Nora are splitting up.

"What's the matter with you?" I yell, furious.

"Jesus Christ, Kerry. It wasn't just me."

"Why can't you make anything work?"

"It's more complicated than that," he says. His voice is even, but I can hear his anger. My own anger sits in my throat like a rock. I know what happened. He doesn't have to tell me. Nora finally had enough.

Later, Nora calls.

"You won't give it another chance?" I ask.

"Honey, your dad's being good to me, considering. He's helping me buy an apartment in New York. But we're not going to be together."

I shake my head, anger at my father creeping up. As usual he's spending money to assuage his guilt. Why doesn't he try to change himself instead?

"We'll stay in good touch," Nora tells me. "You're still my almost daughter."

But I know that's unlikely, and when we hang up, I cry.

◆ ◆ ◆

"WHAT KEEPS YOU in the relationship?" It's our regular weekly session, and Deirdre is asking how things have been with Leif. I haven't told her yet about my father and Nora. I didn't realize why I was so mad at him at first, but since the phone call it's come to me. I'm terrified I'm destined to be like him, happy to have sex but unwilling to go much further.

The tree outside is thick with bright green leaves. It's spring, the time of year I usually feel sexual and alive, when I tend to meet new boys. For the first time I wonder what kind of tree it is. An oak? Spruce? All this time I've come here and I still don't know.

"What is that out there?" I ask. "An oak tree?"

Deirdre follows my gaze to the tree. She looks doubtful. She thinks I'm evading the question.

"Why do you want to know?" She watches me, waiting.

"I'm tired of it," I tell her. "I'm sick of spending all my energy trying to get loved."

An eyebrow raises. "Is that what you're doing?"

"Isn't it?" I want her to give me something here. She's the therapist. *Take this away*, I want to yell. What was I doing here if she wasn't going to change things for me?

"Is that why you're with Leif?" she asks, more questions to answer my questions.

"I don't know," I say, annoyed. "Maybe. Yes."

"And then what?" she asks. "What happens when you get it?"

I shrug. I don't know what she's getting at.

"Kerry," she says. She leans forward, her eyes sharp. "This is where you always are. Trying to get loved. Waiting for something always out of reach."

Tell me something I don't know, I think.

"You just said it yourself. You're missing your life, caught in this place that's neither here nor there."

I listen now.

"What is it that keeps you trapped in this place?" she asks.

I just look at her, unsure.

◆ ◆ ◆

THE SUMMER BEFORE Leif and I will drive out together to Arizona, I go to another writing workshop in New York. This time I feel less anxious about leaving him. I'm excited to throw myself into the writing world again. I have more confidence, too. My story, about a retarded girl who gets gang-raped, was chosen for first prize in my college's short story contest. I've also placed two other stories with small literary magazines. I didn't get in to Arizona, but I plan to move there anyway, maybe take a class or two from the program, write a lot, and apply again. Leif will be starting his program in the fall. Our relationship isn't at its best, but it's secure. We're moving across the country together. That's got to count for something.

The first people I meet when I get to the conference are Melissa and Jen, and instantly the three of us become friends. I tell Jen my story about the three Rachels from high school, and we laugh at our old selves, at the way we cared so much about belonging, even though in many ways I still feel the same way.

Within a day of arriving, there's a boy. His name is Jason. He has dark eyes and messy hair. He smiles shyly when I catch him looking from across the room. He has a girlfriend, whose picture he showed me the first time we spoke, a girl named Leslie with long, curly blond hair.

And, of course, I have a boyfriend. But this doesn't stop me from thinking about him constantly.

At night, when we're in our rooms I fantasize about him coming to me. I imagine a secret blossoming between us, the attraction too strong to control. During the day I try to time it so we'll be in the same place, which isn't easy since he's a poet and I'm a fiction writer. I go for runs on the forest trails surrounding the campus, knowing he runs too, hoping we'll have a chance meeting. For the first time since Leif and I got together, my senses feel sharp, heightened. I'm taken with everything – the way the sun dances against tree leaves, the purple irises lining a walking path. Everything appears rich with life, with meaning.

A few times Jason and I actually talk. Each time it goes something like this:

Him: "How's it going?"
Me: "Pretty good. How about you?"
Him: "Good."

[Ten seconds of uncomfortable silence.]

Me: "You write poetry?"
Him: "Yeah, but I just started. I'm not any good."
Me: "Oh, I'm sure that's not true."
Him: [Looks down at his shuffling feet.]

Me: "I'd love to read some sometime."
Him: [Nervous laughter.]

[More uncomfortable silence.]

Him: "I better get going."
Me: "Sure. Me too."

Jen, who has a class with him, rushes back from her workshop one day to tell me he read a poem called "Temptress." She tries to recount it, an obscure poem about being pulled somewhere he knows he shouldn't go. We squeal and jump up and down. To Jen, my crush is meaningless. She knows I have a boyfriend, who will visit in just a week or so. For me my crush is something more. It allows that old anxiety, the pressure in the air that tells me I might get evidence that I'm worth something. This boy might want me, making me matter. All along I thought being loved by one boy would be enough. Love would free me from my desperation. Here I am, though, no different from when I was a teenager.

Leif visits near the end of the workshop. We have sex in the small twin bed. Our movements are familiar, always the same. His hand on my breast, mine at his back. Then my leg, his neck. My hand goes to his hair, his mouth to my ear. Our kisses could be diagrammed – tongue here, bottom lip there. There are no surprises. The day he leaves, we ride down the elevator together so I can walk him to his car. Our plan is to meet in New Jersey, at my father's apartment, and leave from there for our road trip west.

As we come off the elevator, Jason is there. My heart stops, then picks up tempo. Jason smiles nervously at me and nods at Leif. It is only a moment, but Leif sees it. I can feel the tension as we make our way through the parking lot.

"Do I need to be worried?" he asks when we arrive at his car.

"About what?" I reach for his hand.

"Leaving you here." He squeezes back. "With all these guys."

"Honey." I smile and hug him, smelling his familiar scent. I love him. I do. But like Eli said long ago, I don't know whether that matters. Maybe nothing is ever enough for me. I push away the thought. "You have nothing to worry about," I tell him.

He gets in his car, and I watch him wind his way out of the lot. I walk back to the dorm, anxiety tugging at me. Jason is out there somewhere. How far will I actually go?

The last night of the workshop is the departure reception. I take a breath and go toward Jason. Any fool can see how irrational this is. He's still in college. I'm moving across country. We can barely hold a conversation together. We both have long-term relationships. But I'm not thinking like this. I'm all body. All need. Going to him

239

is only about this moment. It is only about getting to that place inside. That place so many boys have touched, but then it slips away, eluding me again.

Jason smiles, but he also looks around, as though looking for an escape.

"Have I showed you Leslie?" he asks, reaching for his wallet. I stop him with my hand.

"I've seen her," I say.

He looks at me, his mouth tight, and waits.

"You should come by my room tonight," I say quietly.

"Oh, yeah?"

"Yeah."

"Where's your room?"

"Camden Hall. Room 515."

He smiles and nods at a guy nearby. It's one of his friends. I look at the guy and he gives me a funny smile. Jason must have told him about me. About us and this little thing we have.

"Room 515, huh?"

I smile.

"All right," he says. "Maybe I will."

He goes to walk away, and I grab his arm, afraid he won't really come. I quickly try to think of something else to say.

"It will be our little secret" is what I come up with.

Later I lie in bed, waiting. There is a Lorrie Moore story in which the main character waits for her lover to arrive.

She splays her hair just so on the pillow, pulls her nightgown down to reveal cleavage. She holds her position for hours, her back aching from pushing out her breasts, but her lover never comes. In the story, it's funny. But I don't feel humorous right now. I'm leaving tomorrow. Leif and I are about to start a new life in Tucson. I try not to think about that. Instead, I focus on each sound I hear, the elevator door opening and closing, footsteps shuffling along the carpet, voices, water running through pipes. I wait, my eyes open, until four a.m. But just like in the story, Jason never comes.

Ten

THE FIRST WEEK in Tucson, I'm energized. Leif and I find a house to rent, and I land a job in the university bookstore. I wake at seven a.m. every day, leaving Leif in bed, and ride my bike in the frosty air to the store. And when I get home in the early afternoon, the air now warmed by the sun, I try to write. I set up my office in the house, a whole room dedicated to my work. I unpack my books of fiction and books about craft, my *Writer's Market* book and *Handbook of Literary Magazines*. I hang my favorite quote – "Tell me, what will you do with your one wild and precious life?" by Mary Oliver – above my computer. Every other day I go to the gym and do my three-mile run.

But day after day, I can't write. I walk in and out of the office to get more coffee, a snack, to listen to one of Leif's jazz CDs for inspiration. At two thirty, when the mail comes, I perk up, hoping for something good – an acceptance from a literary magazine, a contest win, but usually it's just bills and junk mail.

When Leif comes home, I hang around him while he tries to hash out a composition on the piano.

"Take a walk with me," I plead. Or, "Let's go out for dinner." But he usually shoos me away, wanting to work.

Sometimes, friends he's made in the music program come by, and I sit with them while they talk about scores and changes and composers, and I wish I had friends of my own. Even the bookstore where I work, the one thing I have going, begins to grate on me – all those students with their busy lives, all those people with a purpose.

I call Bevin, who moved to Portland, Oregon, with a few of our friends from college, and complain. She suggests I come for a visit.

My first night there, I meet a boy, and I know my life is about to take a turn.

His name is Zachary. Gorgeous, beautiful Zachary.

At the club where Bevin takes me, Zachary dances up to me, and then against me, his pelvis grinding into mine. Right there on the dance floor he kisses me, a kiss I can feel throughout my body, just like in those first few months with Leif. I know I shouldn't, but I open myself, my body like a hungry flower, gone unwatered for so long. I'm not surprised by myself. Not at all. In fact, I knew it was coming.

Bevin is pissed.

"Kerry," she says when she pulls me aside. "What are you doing?"

"I know." I grin, but Bevin doesn't grin back. "I don't know yet," I say to answer her question.

"What about Leif?" She stares into my face, maybe looking for the girl she thinks I am, not the real me, the one who carelessly flings away her boyfriend's heart.

"I don't know," I say, annoyed now. I don't want to think about it right now. I just want to feel what I've been feeling tonight.

Back at Zachary's house I can barely contain myself. I am lost in the old feeling, all body, all desire, all emptiness. We make it to his bed, but once there, I pull back.

"I have a boyfriend," I say, breathless.

Zachary smiles at me. His eyes are a rich brown. A lock of his blond hair hangs in his face. "What are you saying?" he asks. "Do you want to stop?"

"No." I laugh. "But I should."

Zachary kisses me again. He strips off my shirt and puts his mouth on my breast. I feel like I might explode.

"Whatever you want to do," he says between kisses. He doesn't care. Why should he care?

"Just no sex," I tell him. "Nothing to put my boyfriend at risk."

He doesn't answer, keeps moving down my body.

Such a ridiculous rule. I'm not stupid enough to think this makes it OK.

Back in Tucson, I try to get back into my life. But days when I should be writing, I call Zachary, and when

Zachary isn't available, I call Bevin and ask her about him. With Zachary on my mind I'm permanently aroused. I initiate sex with Leif every night. But nothing, nothing will fill this pit of desire.

Leif notices nothing different, and while this should be a relief, it bothers me.

A few days later, I fly out to my grandparents' condominium in Florida for my mother's second wedding. She has set up a joint celebration with my grandmother's birthday. Donald, who when I first met him was scruffy and dressed in Levi's and T-shirts, is clean-shaven and wearing clothes my mother has picked out for him. He even sounds like her now, discussing art and wine as though these were always his interests.

I'm tempted to tell Mom what I really think, that by controlling Donald she's setting herself up for another fall. But I'm well practiced in keeping my real thoughts and feelings to myself with her, especially when her parents are around. They say things like, "Your mother has worked hard to get to this place," and "Your mother has been through so much." No one's allowed to make Mom feel bad. I just nod and roll my eyes. Silence is still my main line of defense when it comes to her.

I spend most of my time in the clubhouse gym, running on a treadmill, trying not to think.

The day of the wedding, I get drunk. Donald and my mother read vows to each other while Tyler, Donald's two daughters, and I stand beside them. Whenever I glance at Tyler I start giggling, so I will myself to look straight ahead. My uncle toasts them, saying how nice it is to finally see my mother happy again. In many ways, I feel bad for him. Mom's the shining star of that family, the firstborn, which means a great deal in a Jewish family. She can do no wrong. My grandparents approve of everything about her, her taste, her knowledge, her choices in life. All attention goes to my mother, no matter what her brother might do. He is always in her shadow, always the one who should be more like his older sister. Like me, he's always been invisible.

My grandparents, following my mother's lead, eat health food. They collect art and modernist furniture. They believe their choices are superior to others' and that they deserve only the best. But since my uncle's arrival in Florida, he and his family adamantly eat Nathan's hot dogs most every evening, and they make snide comments about my grandparents' "weird" art. If his parents' favoring of my mother hurts him, he refuses to show that. He proudly flaunts how different he is. Maybe I shouldn't feel sorry for him after all.

After the ceremony, Mom gives my grandmother a pendant for her birthday that is supposed to represent a woman's vulva. Grandma shows it off to me when I come over.

"Gorgeous," she says. "Like a cat's eye."

I smile. "It does look like a cat's eye, but it's actually supposed to represent a vagina."

"Really," she says, studying it. "Your mother's something, isn't she? Where does she come up with this stuff?"

"She's a gynecologist," I say, as though this explains anything.

Later, I hear her telling guests who admire it, "Isn't it lovely? Kerry says it's a vagina."

Back in Tucson, I start to itch. My arms, my chest, and my back break out with a strange-looking rash. Leif starts to feel it too. I go to a clinic and leave with a prescription to treat scabies. After I rub on the lotion, I look up scabies on the Internet and learn that little bugs have been living and breeding beneath my skin. Horrified, I scroll down to see how I could have gotten them. Sure enough, they are passed by prolonged skin-to-skin contact or from sleeping in an infected person's bed. I think of everything I've surely infected in the past few weeks. I borrowed a bra from my mother. I slept in my grandparents' guest bed. And of course Leif. I'm repulsed, disgusted with myself. These bugs on me are fitting. I'm a filthy person, dirtying everyone who comes too close.

"So that's what this rash is," Zachary says when I call him.

"How could you not go to a doctor?" I ask. "You've had it longer than I have."

"I figured it would go away."

"Good thing you gave it to me. You would have had it for ages otherwise." I laugh, but only to hide my rage. I haven't forgotten what boys like, the easygoing girl, the girl who doesn't demand too much. I don't want to push him away with my anger, to make him stop wanting me.

He laughs too. "We better have sex soon, in case I have some kind of venereal disease."

"Name the time and place," I say, getting what I wanted.

"How about now?"

Something flutters at my throat. "I'd like that."

"So would I."

When I call Bevin to tell her I plan to say I got the scabies from her bed, she's furious.

"You're making me out to be dirty," she says. "Leif's going to think I'm a slut."

I don't say anything, aware of who's really the dirty slut.

"Fine," she says. "But you owe me big-time."

"You're the best friend ever," I say.

"No," she says, still upset, "I'm not."

My acceptance to the University of Arizona's writing program's spring term arrives the following week. Leif hugs me.

"All right," he says. "This is what you've wanted."

I keep my eyes on the carpeted floor, unable to look at him.

"What?" he asks, his voice changed.

"I think I need to go up to Portland for a while."

"What do you mean?"

"Just until the end of the summer. Then I'll start the writing program in the fall." I peek at him and see the confusion in his face. My heart feels heavy, like a thick stone in my chest.

"Why?" he asks. Tears come into his eyes then. I want to throw something, scream. I don't know what. Mostly, I wish I could cry too, but there's nothing there. Just that thickness moving its way through my body.

"I'm not happy here," I say. Hearing those words, hearing what he must be hearing, I quickly try to think of something else. "And I don't want to start the program midway, when everyone already knows each other."

"That's not what you felt when we first got here. You would have killed to have gotten this acceptance."

I look down again, deflated. The thickness has made its way to my throat, making it hard to speak. "I can't," I manage to say.

The following evening, I pack up my car, and early the next morning, while Leif is still sleeping, I kiss his cheek and leave.

✦ ✦ ✦

ZACHARY AND I spend our first two weeks together in bed, and my condom rule from way back when goes right out the window. I force myself to call Leif, to act like nothing is happening, but our conversations are stilted. I've done irreparable damage.

At the end of those weeks, I walk with Zachary through Safeway and we pass a beautiful girl. I see them look at each other.

"What was that?" I ask.

"What?"

"That look."

"What are you talking about?"

"That look," I say. "I saw you look at that girl."

Zachary shrugs and makes a face, and I can tell immediately I've damaged us now as well.

Later he says, "Maybe you think this is something it isn't."

I look away, sick with myself. Sick of how I ruin everything in my life.

When Leif comes to visit a month later, I try to be enthusiastic. I drive him through the city, stopping at my favorite spots. I want him to see what I already love about Portland, the grassroots feel, the green spaces. But he says it's just an old, industrial city. I touch him constantly, slip my arm through his as we walk, reach for his hand at a café table, wanting things to be the way they were. But he pulls away, or else he passively allows me to do what I want. After I drop him off at the airport, I curl up in bed and stay there the rest of the day. I'm such an idiot. I destroyed everything, pushing away one of the few men who's ever loved me, and for what? For a fling with someone who couldn't care less. A familiar frantic feeling courses through me, and I squeeze my hands into fists. I can't lose him. *I can't lose him.* When I call, though, my heart in my throat, he sounds distant, the full fifteen hundred miles away that he is. He tells me about the girl in his band who picked him up from the airport and surprised him with a plate of bagels at her house. And immediately, I know.

The next time we talk, he confirms it. They've been sleeping together.

Crying, I drive out to see Bevin at work. I don't know what else to do. How else I will live. It is springtime, and flowering trees are at every turn. White and yellow dahlias and blue hydrangeas bloom in people's yards. People walk down the street, laughing. None of it means anything to me. With Leif in my life, I could find other reasons to live. Without him, though, nothing I enjoyed before matters, not my writing, not a lovely summer day, not the stacks of uncracked books in the local bookstore. I grip my stomach, in physical pain from the grief I've caused myself. I'm a hollow shell. I'm nothing.

Bevin, my amazing friend, uses the plane reservation I made months ago, before Leif and I broke up, to visit Tucson so she can gather up the rest of my stuff I left behind. While she is gone, I take early shifts at the juice bar where I work, just so I'll be too tired to think. When I pick her up, I ask her not to tell me anything. She agrees, but when she says nothing I can't stand it.

"Just tell me this," I say. "Did he seem to miss me?"

Bevin doesn't look at me. "He's hurting," she says. "I can tell you that."

"Really?" This part I want to know. "What did he say?"

"He said, 'I don't understand how she could just write me off.' Then he goes, 'Get it? Write me off. She's a writer.' It was really sad."

"But I didn't," I say. "I didn't write him off. He went off with that other girl. I still wanted to make it work." I hear the whine in my voice. I miss him. I want him back. And I feel misunderstood, even though I know there are few other ways to interpret what I did, leaving him like I did. "Do you think I should call him?"

Bevin shakes her head. "I wouldn't." When she sees my face, she adds, "I'm sorry."

A few years later she will explain he was already living with the new girlfriend. Even though he was still hurting, he had moved on. Before I know this, though, I lie in bed and think about what I did. It is still too close to think too much about, the loss too raw. But knowing he hurts makes me feel just a little better. All that time we were together, I got so little from him. I have to wonder if I did this in part to see if he cared. To prove to myself I was loved. I don't like seeing this about myself. It's selfish and insensitive. Worse, it reminds me of something my mother might do, then claim herself as a victim. It's also, of course, what my father did. Rather than just leave the relationship with my mother, he had to do something unconscionable so she had no choice but to want out too. All that sideways communication. How would I ever figure out how to make a relationship work?

When I can't stand thinking about it anymore, I drive out to the coast. Seagulls sit on the craggy rocks. Pines, permanently shaped by the wind, bend into melodramatic forms. I breathe in, listening to the soft, rhythmic sounds of the ocean. In Ecola State Park I tie on my running sneakers and take a jog on the trail. Pine needles fly up beneath my steps. The sun plays patterns on the tree trunks. Birds whistle above me. I don't want to be in pain anymore. I want to be done, to be left unburdened and naked, to tear the hurt off my body like layers of clothes. At the end of the trail I stop and bend forward, hands on my knees, to catch my breath. I'm not healed, but for this moment, I'm better.

◆ ◆ ◆

A NEW FRIEND, Terri, the manager of the juice bar, tries to help me unpack my life. She's twelve years older than me and has been through two divorces. She has wisdom to share. We sit at coffeehouses and discuss my past, how I've made bad choice after bad choice, and the reasons why. When I describe Leif and the ways in which he was emotionally unavailable, hoping to defend my actions, Terri just listens. She sips her coffee and looks at me in a way I've come to recognize will mean she's about to challenge me.

"What about you?" she asks.

"What about me?"

"Whenever I see something flawed about the person I chose, I ask myself how I'm that thing too."

"So, if Leif's unavailable, how am I unavailable too?"

"Exactly," she says.

And I think some more.

Inevitably, though, I get distracted. This time, the distraction's name is Matthew, and he's a chef in the restaurant next to the juice bar. Matthew is big and kind. When we have sex, he lifts my body into the air as though I weigh nothing. But Matthew is in love with someone else, and within two weeks he explains this to me and asks the girl to marry him. Next is Kyle, whom I sleep with on the beach when we get out of town during a heat wave. Then Miles. Then Jack. Then Randy. Each one I hope will be something more than just sex, or at least relieve me of my pain about Leif. And the latter they all do, albeit briefly. In the years following, I will jokingly call this my summer of love. But in truth, there is no love involved at all.

When Leif and I broke up, I applied to MFA programs again, knowing I didn't want to wind up back in Tucson with a broken heart. Now I get acceptance letters, and I decide to go to the University of Oregon, where I've been offered free tuition and a teaching fellowship. So at the end of the summer, I move down to Eugene with Randy's help, and find a small one-bedroom house. The owners planted nasturtium and calendula in the small front yard. There's a lush butterfly bush near the door. It is the first time I've ever lived alone and, starting this new program, I'm hopeful my life will begin to feel better. In the first week, I make a friend, and we go together to a party. Some guy's house.

A boy quickly catches my eye.

Goatee, long hair. We watch each other a while, exchanging smiles. In the kitchen, he approaches me, and when he introduces himself as Dennis, I hear an accent.

"Where are you from?" I ask.

"Germany."

"Your people did terrible things to my people."

He laughs. "You are Jewish?"

"Ostensibly," I say. "Can I say I'm Jewish if I was brought up celebrating Christmas?"

"You can say whatever you want to say."

"Really." I smile, move out of the way while someone reaches behind me for a bottle opener. I think about all the things I'd like to say. I want him to take me home, to kiss me, put his hands on my body. He smiles back. But I don't say anything more.

When I leave that evening, he has my number. So I

wait. By the fourth day, I'm so distracted from my classes, I decide to take initiative. I go to the Modern Languages building where he told me he studies, find his mailbox, and leave a note. "Are you ever going to call? Your creative writing friend." And I write my number again, just in case he lost it.

This time he calls. We set a date, and he shows up at my house with wine and a small bouquet. Within the first hour we're on the floor, peeling off clothes.

"I haven't told you something," Dennis says, pushing my hair from my face.

"Let me guess. You have a girlfriend." I smile, but inside my stomach sinks. Why can I never choose the right guy?

"That's a good guess."

"Then what are you doing?" I ask him.

"Things aren't going well, so we've agreed to take a break and see other people."

I brighten, seeing an opening. As the night progresses, more is revealed. He still lives with her, and he still loves her as well. In the middle of the night, in my bed, he wakes up crying.

"I'm sorry," he says when he leaves. "I'm not ready for this."

But I keep pushing.

I call. I find him at school. We spend more and more time together. And we have more and more sex. Eventually, he moves out, giving me hope. But soon after the move, whenever we have sex, he won't kiss me. He still speaks regularly with his ex-girlfriend. Once, I force a kiss during sex, pulling his face to mine, but he pulls away. The next day, when I ask him what we're doing, he reminds me about the other girl.

"I'm not going to be in love with you when my heart is taken by her," he tells me.

So I move on. Sean, Will, Trent. A few more whose names I forget.

By the time I meet Toby, I'm so far down, so full of desperation, I'd take anyone, *anyone* who will take me too.

We meet when his band comes to a local club. During the band's break we make eye contact. He's very handsome with a broad chest and shoulders that make me feel like maybe he could protect me. We spend the night in my apartment, and I travel the two hours to see him every weekend after.

Toby works for a contractor repairing and restoring boats, but what he really wants to do is animation. He shows me reams of paper on which he's drawn characters smoking weed and plucking buds off plants. I know he does bong hits throughout the day. But until he opens up his closet to show me an elaborate setup of five marijuana plants, I don't realize this is his passion as well. He takes me to see three other places, in hidden meadows, where he's planted eight more. The stacks of twenties I see around his room, money I naively thought he earned at work, begins to make more sense.

Back at school, with Toby choosing to be with me, I focus once more on my writing. I bang out story after story. One I land in a well-known literary magazine. Another my professor chooses for an anthology. The discussions about writing that I engage in with my colleagues excite me. Ideas about form and narrative. I gather a new language with which to talk about my and others' work, a language highly intellectual and academic. On the weekends, though, I drop all of that so I can be with Toby.

Not that we talk about much anyway. Mostly we just have sex. Good, hot sex.

When the program comes to an end, Toby and I find a place to rent in a Portland suburb. I set up an office for writing and start teaching at a local college. Toby sets up his plants. And very quickly, things begin to disintegrate.

First, Toby gets kicked out of the band. Then he loses his job. My adjunct positions don't make enough to carry us, so he takes various day-long warehouse jobs through a temp agency, making close to minimum wage. Anytime I try to talk to him about getting a real job, he gets hurt and defensive. I know from watching my own father that job issues are hard for men. They cut straight to their sense of self. So I learn not to talk about it at all. He also starts smoking more. Almost every day I come home from teaching to find him in front of the TV with the bong. After I express my dismay a few times, he starts relegating himself to the basement. Often, as I open the front door, I see a flash as he races to get down there, away from me and what he will call my "constant judgment." At night, he goes out with friends, leaving me steaming and alone.

I call Bevin, who has moved back East, and vent. Terri and I meet and analyze the situation. The bottom line, though, doesn't take a whole lot of analysis. I shouldn't be with him. I know that. I'm not stupid. Yet I make no moves. I tell a friend, "If I weren't so damn attracted to him, maybe I would leave." And this is true. But I don't tell her the real problem. There's something deeply wrong with me if I'm so attracted to someone who can't have a relationship, someone who can't love me, who can't even love himself. I've learned at this point there's no shot I can receive, no pill I can take, no therapy I can be a part of that will give me the resolve to do the things I need to do to be loved. It's a choice. A simple choice. I say I want intimacy. I say I want to be loved. But really, I'm petrified. The straight truth is, I don't know if I have it in me, and I'm scared to find out that I can't.

When Toby gets home and into bed, he wraps his arms around me.

"Please don't leave," he says.

"I'm sleeping," I mumble. "I'm not going anywhere."

"I mean it," he says. "I'd die without you."

"Don't be crazy."

"I wouldn't survive."

Long after he starts snoring, I lie awake, unable to get back to sleep.

One morning I wake up, sure I am pregnant. I've had pregnancy scares in the past, when I've had unprotected sex at random times during my cycle. But this is different. It's a knowledge. It sits against my throat, making me gag when I brush my teeth. A month earlier I tried going off the Pill. While I struggled to own my body emotionally, I thought I could at least try to reclaim it physically in this small way. I wanted to know my body better, to get it back. So I tried tracking my cycles. But I screwed up somewhere. I know that now, looking at myself in the mirror, my eyes wide.

I call Mom and leave her a message. I pace the apartment, wanting the phone to ring. I think about Toby, how I don't want a baby right now. I don't want to go through an abortion either. I know too many friends who had them, what a big deal it was. I don't want any big deals. Big emotions. I don't want any of that. Another knowledge flashes through my mind – I don't want a baby with Toby – but I push it away. When the phone rings, I answer it on the first half-ring.

"Where are you in your cycle?" Mom asks when I tell her. She is all business, and right now I appreciate it. I don't want to talk about anything emotional.

I tell her I'm right at the end.

"Too late for the morning-after pill," she says.

I press a hand to my forehead, scared.

"There's something else we can do. A little secret of gynecologists."

"I'll do anything," I say.

She prescribes a special package of pills and gives me the formula: one pill the first night. Two the next. Three the next. And so on until they're all gone.

The first night is fine. The next, I wake in the middle of the night and puke. The third, I'm so nauseous and exhausted from vomiting, I think I might die.

"I can't do this," I tell Mom.

"OK," she says. "We'll try something else."

She prescribes a different pill I'm to take for ten days. On the first night, I cramp so badly I have to crawl to the bathroom, thinking I might throw up again. But the next night nothing happens. And on the seventh day I begin to bleed.

I sit on the couch, holding a hot water bottle against my belly. Toby and his friend are in the basement, getting high. After an hour or so I hear him call from the side door.

"I'm going out."

I throw the bottle toward the door. It falls with a thud to the floor like something dead.

Nine months into the relationship, I drag Toby with me to a couples' therapist. We sit on the soft couch in her office and hold hands, afraid. I tell her about Toby's distance, his pot smoking, his inability to hold a real job. I don't mention his selling because Toby warned me not to. And I don't mention what I just found out recently.

Toby sometimes has sex with men when he goes to clubs, but he doesn't know I know. A friend of a friend who does the same thing told me. The therapist, an overweight middle-aged woman, nods and writes in her pad. When she asks Toby to talk, he says he's tired of me always hounding and judging him and not accepting him for who he is. The therapist wraps up by explaining Toby is an addict and I'm codependent, fitting us into neat compartments. She tells a story about her own son who is an alcoholic and how eventually she had to make the decision to cut him out of her life. She tears up, and with the tears wobbling in her eyes, she looks right at me.

"You need to leave him," she says. "And when you do, you will need me. So let's schedule a session for just you and me."

Toby looks down, probably thinking I will agree. "I'll think about it," I say, icy.

And I search for another therapist. I don't want a therapist who clings to the same tired, old narratives about people and their tendencies. I want someone who can think beyond the obvious. I want someone brilliant. I want someone who, at the very least, will just listen, let me arrive at my own pace to what I already know.

So I find one for just me. The first time I see her, I immediately like her. Not because she strikes me as extremely competent. Not because she doesn't talk about her own life, though if she had, this would have been a deal breaker after the last one. I like her because she reminds me of Nora. Something about her expressions, and her calculator that is studded with sequins. I feel mothered by her. In our first sessions I talk about my parents and childhood. But by the third session, she wants to know more about Toby.

"You're a creative, ambitious woman with a future," she says. "What are you doing with this guy?"

"He's not that bad," I say defensively. "I know he loves me."

"Really?" she asks. "How?"

I don't tell her about his midnight confessions, how he'd die without me. Besides, I know, love songs aside, not being able to live without someone is not love. It's need. "Because he says so," I say, just to answer her question.

She eyes me doubtfully.

"Relationships are supposed to be hard," I say. "They take work."

"True," she says. "But they aren't supposed to be *this* hard."

Many days, I go to Terri's apartment and hang out. We drink tea and talk. A different person might get frustrated with my inertia, but Terri enjoys dissecting the problem and helping me find answers. She isn't looking to fix me, just to help me find my way out.

"He's your father," she tells me. "A pot addict and escapist, but also needy."

I remember the time my father got into bed with me, how it felt too close. I know he wasn't trying to be sexual. I knew that then, too. But his need was so big and careless, taking up space in my bed. Just like my mother's. And Toby's. Need and sex have always been confused for me.

I sigh and look out the window. Outside a studio apartment in the building across the street I see a for rent sign.

"I'm getting tired of it," I admit.

❖ ❖ ❖

THAT WINTER, TOBY and I fly to St. Louis where Tyler and Gill host Christmas. My dad meets us there too. It is the first time I visit Tyler there, and as soon as I step into the house I feel bothered. I can't tell what it is, whether too many knickknacks and books fill the space too tightly, or the windows don't let in enough light. Tyler is dampened, deadened. She moves slowly through the room as though being careful not to fall. She's hard pressed to smile, and when she does it's slow, measured. It doesn't reach her eyes. I know she had begun to act like this when we were teenagers, after Mom left, but it's worse now. A lot worse. It hurts my heart to think of who she was as a child, always jumping and twirling with energy. I used to watch her do the things I was too afraid to do, like swing upside down on the jungle gym or climb the apple tree in our backyard, my heart heavy with admiration and love. I would do anything for her if it meant she would give me just a little of her attention. I don't show her, but my love for her is still fierce and unconditional, the way it is with all little sisters.

Toby brings weed for my father, and within a few hours of his arrival they step outside to smoke together. Terri's observation hangs in the air, weighing it down even further, and by the time Toby and I are alone, I'm furious.

"I don't appreciate you being my father's drug dealer," I say as I make the guest bed with the sheets Tyler left out.

"Here we go again." He stands at the doorway, his arms crossed.

"You don't get it." I jam the corners of the sheet under the mattress. "This isn't about you smoking your fucking pot. It's about your total and utter insensitivity to me. You know how I felt growing up with him, how it felt like he was barely there."

"Could we not have one of your therapy talks right now?" he says. "I'm on vacation."

"Vacation from what?"

His jaw tightens. "Fuck you," he says, and he walks out of the room.

I sit on the bed, tears in my eyes. I want to be compassionate. I really do. Toby told me stories about his childhood. His mother was mentally ill and refused to take medication. Toby came home from school each day afraid of what he'd find. Sometimes he'd find her rocking in her bed, speaking unintelligibly. For weeks at a time he lived on saltine crackers because his mother spent her Social Security checks on clothes or jewelry. Once she held a knife to her wrists and yelled, "You don't love me!" again and again while he crouched, terrified, in the corner. Toby's father, who left them when Toby was a baby, didn't return Toby's calls. In many ways I understand why he smokes so much. The pain of living can be unbearable for someone like him. My life wasn't nearly as awful as his, but I know what it's like to feel you have no parents, no roots to anchor you to the earth.

I feel sorry for Toby, perhaps more so than loving him.

A few days into our visit, Tyler and Gill get sick with the flu. That heaviness in the air grows even thicker, and I'm desperate to get home. But the day we're finally supposed to leave, an ice storm hits Portland, and the airport closes. Toby and I watch TV. We take walks in the neighborhood, passing the boxy brick houses that all look the same. Every few hours I call the airline, trying to work out how to get home. I bounce my knee. I can't keep my hands still. By the time we get to the airport, the flights to Portland jammed with people whose flights were canceled, my anxiety about being trapped is so high that I feel like I'm going to cry.

When we finally get home on New Year's Eve, five days later than planned, I'm resolute. I can't stay in this relationship anymore.

Three weeks later, I move my stuff into the apartment across the street from Terri.

My therapist is thrilled.

"This is a good first step," she says. "Now you can begin to do some real work."

I nod, but I don't tell her the whole truth. I still sleep with Toby every couple of weeks. I've also been sleeping with another guy, a boy from Tennessee who makes me beg to have sex with him and only sometimes acquiesces, who tells me I'm too sexual for him and I should really tone it down. I don't want her to know the truth. I'm too ashamed by my weakness, my inability to sit with my pain.

One afternoon, Toby and I see Steven Spielberg's *Amistad,* and afterward Toby wants to eat. The plan is we'll walk back to my apartment where I'll wash my face since the movie made me cry, and then take his car to La Señorita for burritos. But by the time we get to my apartment, Toby says he's too hungry to wait for me to run in.

"I'll be two minutes," I say. "Just let me wash up."

"Do what you want," he says, his tone biting and mean. "I'm going."

Enraged, I get in the car with him.

"I can't believe what an asshole you are," I say.

"I have low blood sugar." He pulls the car into the street and stops with a jerk at the stop sign.

"Then carry peanuts with you," I say. "What are you, a child? If you know you have low blood sugar, grow up and take care of yourself."

"I'm not going to have this conversation," he says.

"Yes, you are." I yank down the window, letting the cool air in. "If you can't wait for two fucking minutes for me to do something for myself, then you're going to listen to my anger about it this whole car ride."

"Get the hell out of my car," he yells as we come to a red light.

And suddenly it hits me. I don't have to do this anymore. I left. Months ago. Yet here I am, allowing the same crap I allowed for too long.

"OK," I say, my voice calm now. "I will." I open the door and get out of the car. I walk away from Toby for good.

PART THREE

Enough

Eleven

IN MY SMALL studio, I begin my new life without him. I buy two bookcases for my books and a low-maintenance plant. I paint the bathroom sky blue and the kitchen a rich red. I take a kickboxing class. I teach four writing classes and work on the novel I've been meaning to write since I finished my MFA. Four writer friends and I meet regularly to critique one another's work. Spring comes again. Cherry blossoms fill the trees, dropping their pink petals to the ground below. The air grows sweet and heady with the scent of flowers. People emerge from their homes, eyes bright, skin pale from the months of rain, and roam the streets. I feel their hunger, their readiness for something new and exciting. Or maybe that's just me.

My writer friends and I go to bars and to see live music.

And my parade of boys continues.

First, Homeless. A friend names him this for his long, unkempt hair. He sits on my bed talking for hours about the organic farm he plans to run someday while I wait for us to have sex. A week later, when I run into him, he introduces me to his friend as Sarah. Then Eurhythmy, a boy who can sound out words through dance. He practices dance moves in a white robe, the official uniform of eurhythmy dancers. During my time with Eurhythmy, one of my friends tells me he tried to order a Big Mac in eurhythmy, but they turned him away.

"I don't understand," he had said. "I was wearing the robe and everything."

Next is Hold the Phone – he says this to me during sex because he doesn't want to come too soon. Another friend says "hold the phone" every time she makes me wait on the line while she answers her call-waiting.

We laugh and laugh.

When I'm with these boys, I'm still caught up with wanting more, hoping they'll love me. But I have to admit, I'm beginning to see the humor.

Somewhere in all of this, I decide to contact Leif. Thinking about my relationship with Toby and how I reached that low point brings me back to him, how I never really got over what happened between us. All this time, I've never found a way to close the space he occupies in my heart. The fact is, I still love him.

Leif is surprised to hear from me. We chat gregariously for a half hour, and then I ask if I can visit. I didn't plan to ask, but now that we're talking, I feel how much I miss him. He's not seeing anyone, and neither am I. Maybe there's a chance we could make things work again.

"Why?" he asks.

"Because I'd like to see you." I bite the inside of my cheek, nervous.

"I don't know."

I wait, my heart heavy. I caused his reluctance, I know. But it feels awful he isn't as anxious to see me as I am to see him.

"I can come next month," I say. "Just a couple days."

"You really want to come."

"I do."

"OK," he says. "Let me know when you get the ticket."

The week before I leave, Terri comes over and helps me pack. She lends me a black slip dress, which I try on before I put it in my suitcase.

"Do you think he'll be attracted?" I ask. I turn to look at my butt, which always looks big to me, no matter what I'm wearing.

"Is he blind?" she asks back. She sits on my bed, holding the glass of wine I poured for her.

I laugh. "I'm so nervous," I say. I pull the dress over my head, not wanting to think anymore about what I'll look like to him, whether he'll still think I'm pretty. "Why am I so fucking nervous?"

"You haven't seen him in two years," she says. She hands me the glass of wine. "That's a long time when you still love someone."

"I want him to still love me."

"Just get down there," she says. "You'll get your answers when you're with him."

When the plane lands in Tucson, I powder any shine off my face. I reapply lip gloss and fluff up my hair. Then I walk with the other passengers into the terminal. Everyone hugs and exclaims. But Leif isn't there. I walk toward baggage claim. I look out the doors to see if he's waiting in his car. But he's nowhere. After everyone else on my flight is long gone, I go to a pay phone and dial his number, but there's no answer. I sit against the wall and try to decide what to do. Just as I stand to try to call him again, I see him loping up the stairs. The same goofy walk he always had, his dark hair shining under the airport's fluorescent lights. Soon after we first got together he told me he was a human "L" because of his long feet and short stature. My heart fills.

"I'm sorry," he says. "I ran a little late."

I hug him, his scent, that same familiar scent, surrounding me.

"You look good," I say. "I like the hair." I rustle his hair, which is cut short now.

"Yeah?" He touches his hair, and I see in the gesture his insecurity. He feels like I do, nervous and uncertain about how this will go.

I follow him out to his car, not the one he had when I left him, but a van. I watch him as he drives, my Leif, no longer mine with his new hair, his new van. At his apartment, where he lives with one other guy who isn't there this weekend, he pulls me into another hug. We hold each other a moment, just feeling that after all this time. In his bedroom, there's a framed photograph of him and a girl. A pretty girl. They're both tan, their smiles big. Another photo shows him and the same girl from behind as they run hand-in-hand into the ocean.

"That's in Nogales," he says. "It's only an hour's drive from here."

"Who is this?" I ask. I don't look at him, not wanting him to see me. Jealousy's such an ugly emotion.

"Sarah," he says. "We went out for a year after the girl from the band." I watch him look at the picture, trying to gauge what he feels.

"Were you in love with her?"

"Yeah."

I sit on his bed and take off my shoes.

"Let's have sex," I say.

"What?" He laughs, uncomfortable, but his eyes are on me now, not the photo.

I lift my shirt and I set it aside. Underneath I'm not wearing a bra. Then I stand and unbutton my jeans. "Come here."

He does, and I reach for him. I yank off his shirt, and then his pants. I pull him on top of me, my mouth on his. He gets inside of me, but still it's not close enough. I want to feel him again. To know him, like I used to, the last two years – and that girl – erased. I want things back to what they were, when I didn't question whether he was mine. But it's different. Little things. The way he touches me down there. The way he moves. I don't recognize our sex as ours. I used to feel so bored with the predictability of our sex, but now I long for its familiarity, to feel that we still know each other so intimately.

Late in the afternoon, we drive up into the Catalina Mountains. As the road ascends, saguaro cacti give way to Arizona oak and Douglas fir trees. In the distance, the range's sandy slopes, lined with wind and water erosion, look like a woman's curves. The afternoon sun sends shoots of orangey light onto the road. This is where I had planned to live, among the southwest's dusty, airy landscape. Ever since my father and I traveled to Taos, I was sure I belonged here. Now it belongs to Leif. For the first time I see the meaning. Leif applied to the school here after he knew I wanted to come. He came out here to be with me.

We set up camp on a raised ridge where we watch the sun sink into a ravine. It's too warm for a fire, but he makes one anyway, and he opens a bottle of beer for me.

"So, here you are," he says, and he raises his bottle.

"Here I am." I clink his with mine.

"I didn't think you'd ever come back."

I take a breath. "Sometimes I wish I never left."

"Why did you?"

"I don't know," I say. I watch him, wanting to say the

right thing. "I was confused. I needed to get out of here for a while and find something else." He looks up at the star-filled sky while I talk. I can't tell what he's thinking. I want to make this better, to tell him the truth after all this time, but I'm not even sure what that is. "It wasn't about you. I was empty, and no one, not even you, could have filled me."

He looks back at me now, and I see he's crying. After all this time, he's crying. "You just left me."

My throat clenches. I see what I've done, how much I've hurt him, this man I care for. "Oh, God, Leif," I say. "I'm so sorry." I get up and hold him, and he sobs like a little boy in my arms. "I wish I could take it back." I really, really do.

The next night I watch his band perform at a bar, and I see how settled he is here. He has friends and flirtations. People know him as Sarah's ex, not my ex. They don't know me at all. The following morning, Leif drives me to the airport and we hug good-bye. I've been a fool in the past. That's for sure. But I'm not disillusioned enough to think we'll be together now. He has a whole life he's happy in, and his life no longer includes me.

◆ ◆ ◆

AT THE END of July, I fly across the country to attend an artists' colony in Vermont. I fly into New Jersey, where I'll see my dad for a day and pick up a car. Then I'll drive to the Berkshires to see my grandmother, who is alone since my grandfather passed, and finally to see Bevin before I head up to Vermont. On the flight over, I sit next to a handsome, well-groomed boy. Three hours into it, we make out. I can see by the little tent in his pants that he'd like us to do more. I briefly consider jerking him off under the tiny airline blanket, but he doesn't push for it, so I don't offer. We exchange numbers, but he lives in Philadelphia, and I'm on a tight schedule this trip. I know I won't see him again.

Dad takes his new girlfriend and me out for dinner at an Italian restaurant we went to often when I lived here. Perhaps it's the familiarity of the place that leads me to tell his girlfriend about the things Dad did when I was a teenager. Or perhaps it's been brewing inside me too long. Over dessert and coffee, I tell her how he used to make sexually suggestive comments about my friends, be inappropriate in front of me with his girlfriend, and smoke pot with my friends. With each debasement I mention, she slaps Dad hard on the arm.

"What's wrong with you?" she says with play anger.

He laughs uncomfortably. "It was years ago." And then, "Check, please."

"You can't run from your past," I tell him, and smile.

"Maybe not," he says. "But I don't have to sit here and take this abuse."

"Yes, you do," his girlfriend says.

The waiter places the check on the table.

"Everything was OK?" he asks.

"Everything but the food and company," Dad says, his standard joke.

"And you have to pay for our dinner after we abuse you," his girlfriend says after the waiter walks away. I smile, thinking of Nora and her list of what men are good for. I guess Dad likes this sort of teasing from his women. I know inside he believes it's true. He has to do things for the women in his life to be worthy of them, to make up for all his mistakes.

Dad gets his wallet out. He shakes his head and laughs while he pulls out an American Express. "That's right," he says. "I'll never be paid up, will I?"

I just laugh and raise my eyebrows. That's for him to determine.

His girlfriend goes to bed early, and Dad and I sit in the living room. He turns on the TV and lights a cigarette, his two biggest vices. He's too old to still be smoking and though I shouldn't encourage him, I light one too.

"What really happened with Nora?" I ask.

Dad sighs. He leans back and blows out smoke in a thin stream. "A lot of things happened," he says. "You know how relationships go."

I do. "What sorts of things?"

"For one, she drank too much."

"Really?" Images of Nora come back to me, the glass of

wine always in her hand. And the night they came home, her weird looseness, her breath reeking. "I guess I never understood that."

"I didn't feel you had to know."

I nod, appreciating he thought to protect me like that.

"There were other things. Her insecurity. My immaturity." He smiles.

"You're getting pretty old to be pleading immaturity," I tell him.

He smiles again. "True story."

"So what about this one?" I nod my head in the direction of his bedroom. "Are you feeling more mature?"

He raises his eyebrows, looks toward the TV a moment. "Let's just say I don't expect her to be perfect this time."

"So you are more mature."

"Maybe I am."

Later I find my senior high school yearbook and sit on my childhood bed. In my picture I gaze out at the camera, not smiling. My makeup is too heavy, my nails bitten down and ragged. It's easy to see how unhappy I was, why I made all those bad choices I did with the boys in Manhattan and with Heath and the Rachels. I flip through the rest of the book, looking for myself there. My classmates fill the pages, playing soccer and volleyball, performing in plays. They look happy, involved. But I'm nowhere to be found. I close the book and put it away, sadness filling my chest. I want to believe I'm different now. I've overcome the pain that made me act so impulsively and harmfully. But I don't really know if that's the case.

◆ ◆ ◆

AFTER I SPEND time with Bevin, I start my retreat in Vermont. The summer here is hot. The landscape is lush and green. Birds lazily circle overhead. Crisp river water rushes by beneath a bridge. Days, I work on my novel. When I grow restless, I walk in the warm sun down to the main house, hoping to find others procrastinating too. Or I head up to the gym in the college nearby and run on the treadmill. There aren't any boys for me here, but it's one of those rare times I'm OK with this. I like the friends I've made, especially three painters – all guys – with whom I go to the local bar some nights. We shoot pool or sit with beers and cigarettes and discuss music and art. I'm attracted to one, Frank, who has sharp blue eyes and skin around them that crinkles when he smiles, but he's married, so I don't go there.

The first week, Frank and Jerry, another painter, and I go to the bar, which is two miles away in the next town. Locals play pool and classic rock sails down from overhead speakers. When I order wine, the bartender, a scruffy man with a big belly, laughs at me and then calls into the back for someone to find the box of Franzia. Frank laughs at me too.

"You don't come from a place like this, do you?"

"And you do?" I smile.

"I know my way around a dive bar."

"Maybe that isn't something to be so proud of." I light a cigarette. I can feel those blue eyes on me, the way he's watching my mouth. Jerry gets up to watch the pool game, maybe feeling something happening he doesn't want to be a part of.

"You think you're so smart, writer girl," Frank says.

"I do."

He pulls a cigarette from my pack, and we both watch as it comes out.

"You have paint on your hand," I tell him.

"That's because I paint." He smiles, watching me watch his hand. He lights the cigarette.

"It's sexy," I say.

He leans toward me. "You," he says in a low voice, "are a very dangerous girl."

During the week, after a few hours of writing, I go to find him painting outside on the bank of the river. We sit together in the sun and talk seriously about our work. Two days before I'm to leave, during one of these times by the river, he tells me he's crazy about me. At first, I try just to be flattered. I like him, too – a lot. But he's married. This guy is married. Somewhere his wife is going about her day, assuming Frank is in Vermont, innocently painting away. Perhaps she rushes home every afternoon, checking to see whether he's called. Perhaps she would never consider that he's hitting on me, that rather than thinking of her when he's alone in his bed he's thinking about what it would feel like to touch me. But as the minutes pass, as we sit together and talk about this thing that could never be, as he explains how different I am from his wife, how much he learns from our discussions, how he loves the way I see things, a familiar feeling rears its head inside: There's another woman, and he chooses me.

Later, we go swimming in a nearby river with some other friends. The water is icy cold, but I barely feel it. I'm too aware now of Frank, of whether he's looking at me, thinking of me. I'm too aware of me.

In the evening, we sit in the dark on a stoop and kiss. He pulls himself back, then comes toward me again, grappling with himself. He's drunk. I know he had to drink to be able to be with me like this. Sober, he's thinking of his marriage. He tells me he thinks he got married too young, and now he doesn't know what he wants. I want him to decide he wants me.

The final night we all have a party, and Frank and I dance together in the corner of the room. We're both tipsy, and I can feel how dangerous our dancing is, how our hips press against each other's, our breath near each other's ears. A little later a girl asks me, "What's going on with you and Frank?" I can see the excitement in her eyes. Artist colonies are notorious for breaking up marriages and housing affairs. They're also breeding grounds for gossip, usually about those affairs, probably because making art is such a painfully introspective and lonely business, and gossip gets you out of yourself. Hence the girl's excitement. But I say, "Nothing," and make a face to suggest she's being silly. If Frank knew people were talking he'd surely pull away.

I wind up in his bed, but he won't touch me. He tells me he'll miss me. I want badly for him to put his hands on me, to feel evidence of his wanting me. It's such an old habit. How easily I'm pulled right back to that place, where I am only body and desperation, where everything depends on this one man's decision. *Will he love me? Will he not love me?* I try to talk myself down, to realize that this is also enough, just knowing he wants it as much as I do.

When I leave, I tell myself it's over, but he calls me the next night.

"I can't stop thinking of you," he says.

"I wish I were still there."

"I do too. But I'm also glad you're not. I'm afraid of what would happen."

"You wouldn't be able to resist me." I laugh, joking, but I want him to agree.

"Maybe."

"You should come here," I tell him. "Just do it."

I hear him breathing. "I can't. Not now."

I bite my lip, wishing I had magic words to get him to join me.

"But I want to," he adds.

I buy a CD he tells me to buy. Palace Music. It's romantic, heartbreaking, angst-ridden. I make a CD for him with Richard Buckner's "Once" where he sings about wishing to be saved and Aimee Mann's "Save Me." It's true. I want to be saved from myself, from my hurting. I want a boy like Frank to lift me up like a dead thing and breathe me into life. I lie on my bed in my little studio and feel how badly I want Frank with me. How I want his interest in me to mean something, to mean I'm worth something as big as ending his marriage. It's so selfish, I know. Some time later, when I'm married myself, I'll know just how selfish. After years of tangling your lives, of making compromises and concessions, of building a shared life, it's appalling to imagine someone else, some outside person, dismissing all of this for her own gain. But I don't think of any of that now. I feel the wanting in my bone marrow. It's like a nasty virus that won't die.

The next time we talk, I try another tactic.

"You got married so young," I tell him. "It's reasonable to grow in different directions."

"I know," he says. "But she loves me. I still love her. It's not so simple."

"But you're unhappy."

"How do I know I won't be unhappy if I leave her?"

"You can't know unless you take the risk. If you stay, though, you're just unhappy."

He sighs.

I sigh too. "I don't like this," I tell him. "Being the other woman. I thought I was too smart for this."

"I understand." He's quiet a moment. "You shouldn't be, then. Don't wait for me, Kerry. I'm lost right now."

I tell my therapist he said this.

"Sounds like he's being honest," she says.

"But he sounded so unhappy saying it."

"He probably was."

I look down at my foot, which I kick lightly against the coffee table that separates us.

"He likes me for who I am," I tell her, hearing the whine in my voice. "Nobody's ever really seen me like that before."

She cocks her head, waiting.

"I'm such a cliché, aren't I, waiting for him to leave his wife? I can't believe this is me."

She smiles. "No one's a cliché," she says as she tucks a strand of her straight blond hair behind an ear. "We all have to go through our own unique experiences, and we all have to find our own unique ways out."

I look at her bookshelf, full of self-help books and psychopathology texts, and consider this. "How am I supposed to get out?" I ask.

"The way to get out is always the way you came in," she says and smiles.

A few days later, I get a call from Tyler.

"I left him," she says.

"Gill?"

"I couldn't do it anymore."

And then it all comes pouring out. How Gill has been going on out-of-control shopping sprees, buying elaborate trips to foreign countries without consulting her. When she's dared to confront him he's become belligerent and self-righteous. Other times he does nothing but sulk or lie in bed for hours.

"I'm in San Francisco," she says. "With someone else."

"So that's it?" I ask. "You just left everything? The house, all your stuff? And you left with another man?"

Tyler's silent. She knows what I'm thinking. She's not dealing with her life.

"I just needed out," she says quietly. "Being married to Gill was like being married to Mom. I couldn't separate his needs from my own. I was dying there, Kerry."

I close my eyes. Tyler was Mom's stand-in husband for so long, it makes sense she wound up marrying someone who made her feel the same way. I want to be kind, to listen and be helpful, but I'm angry and I'm not sure why.

"What about Gill?" I ask. "Have you talked to him?"

"I can't."

When I don't say anything, she says, "I'm going to have to do this my way, Kerry. I know what I did. But it hasn't been easy for me, either."

I think of Leif, the mistakes I made. I don't want her

making the same mistakes. But I hear her. She's my sister and she needs me. That's all that matters. "OK," I say. "I get it."

The next week, Gill calls.

"Come with me to Venezuela," he says. "Just you and me."

"What are you talking about?"

"I'm going next month. Come on. We'll have fun."

"Gill," I say. "We're not even friends. You don't know me."

"I've always loved you."

"You're manic," I say. "Do you have anyone there to help you?"

"I don't need help," he says, angry now.

"I'm going to go," I tell him. "I'm going to call your parents and have them go over there."

"Don't you dare," he says right before I hang up.

I call Tyler, who promises she'll get a hold of his parents, and when we get off the phone I call Terri to come over. I don't want to be alone, knowing Gill is somewhere out there, feeling so much pain.

The next time Tyler and I talk, she mentions Dad's five-year affair.

"Hold on," I say. "Dad had an affair on Mom for five years?"

"I thought you knew that."

"Mom told you things, not me." I look out the window of my small kitchen, feeling the old jealousy.

"You didn't want to hear them." Tyler's voice is full of pain too. She's had her own difficult road, I'm well aware. She's the one who had to bear Mom's grown-up burdens, perhaps because I wouldn't.

I take a deep breath. Our parents pitted us against each other, but I don't want to play that game anymore. We're supposed to be adults now, directing our own lives. "Was it the same woman for all five years?"

"I think so. Remember Lynn?"

I close my eyes, searching my memory for a Lynn.

"She worked with him."

I get a flash then, a slender woman with tight, dark hair. Standing in an unfamiliar kitchen. "Maybe," I say.

"It was over pretty soon after the divorce."

"So much for the idyllic childhood Mom wants us to remember."

Tyler laughs. Maybe it's because we've both made grown-up mistakes at this point too, but we can do this now. We can poke fun at both parents without feeling we have to protect them so much.

On a jog later I think about the few memories I have before the divorce, the fun parties, staying up late, all of Mom and Dad's friends. If I angle the camera just slightly, I think maybe I can see it: Mom's forced smiles, Dad's unhappy gaze turned away. In the revisions I find I feel sorry for them. Like in that Sharon Olds poem, "I Go Back to May 1937," where she wishes she could warn her parents of all the mistakes they'll make, all the pain they'll suffer and inflict. I wish I could go back, too. I wish I could tell them to change it all, to start over, to think more about what they're both about to do.

Friends and I go out to bars, and I meet a few more boys. I do my usual smiling across a room. I talk with them about whatever they're eager to talk about. But I find myself bored. Even during the sex. I turn my head to the side, wondering why I'm doing this. Why I'm still doing this, after so many years.

When Frank calls, the caller ID screen says unavailable, like some kind of mean joke.

I make a tentative decision: No more boys for a while. Just to see what will happen.

Days pass. I spend time with my friends. I teach. I read novels and work on my own. I even try reading a self-help book about how to find love. The gist is that when you can love yourself entirely, only then can others love you too. Duh. Any moron knows that. But *how* to love yourself after a lifetime of self-degradation and effacement? That would be a book worth reading. I call Leif at some point, just to hear how he is and to wish him well. I miss him still. Some days, I sit in my small apartment with my loneliness, an unwanted guest, the pain intense enough that I keep my arms wrapped around my middle. I can almost envision it in there – a tiny girl with dead eyes, sitting alone in the dark. I hold her tightly, trying to bring her back to life. On these days, I don't want a boy. Being alone feels more honest.

A few times I go out to solo dinners at a sidewalk café and watch people walk by. I see a movie by myself and cry the whole way through. A few people glance at me, but I don't care. I don't have to answer to anyone, and that feels nice.

I joke with my friends about what I'm doing, calling it a moratorium on my vagina. But it's actually quite serious. I've crossed a threshold somewhere. We all have the opportunity to find that place where awareness trumps our actions. And I've reached that place. I can't go back.

◆ ◆ ◆

I FLY TO visit Mom. In the Art Institute of Chicago's café, the café that has the same installation of small kites as she has in her home, she tells me she and Donald are getting divorced. Angrily, she explains Donald has been seeing another woman. She tears up as she speaks, obviously in pain, obviously resigned.

"I did so much for him," she says. "He just changed all of a sudden. I don't know him anymore."

For the first time ever, I feel sorry for her. I put my hand on hers. "I'm sorry, Mom."

"I don't understand what happened."

I think of Terri's words about the people we choose,

how they're mirrors of ourselves. I want to say something about this, but I'm afraid she'll misunderstand.

"I never liked Donald," I say instead.

"You didn't?"

"He was spineless. He allowed you to turn him into whoever you needed him to be."

"That's not true. We just had the same taste."

I sigh, knowing we won't see eye to eye.

"Either way," I say, "I'm sorry this is happening."

She looks down at her coffee. "Me too."

That evening, lying awake in her guest room, I think about her – how, like me, she doesn't know how to keep love in her life. It pains me to think of her like this, lost and wanting, desperate for love. She's gone so far into her life, and yet she's still like a child, tugging on sleeves, pushing people over, trying so very hard to get what she needs. I'm like that too, aren't I? That little girl inside, clawing her way through life, wanting, always wanting, never ever getting enough to feel filled. It's so ugly. So profoundly sad and ugly. I don't want to be like this anymore.

◆ ◆ ◆

BACK HOME, I go out a few times with friends, testing the waters. In a bar, there's a boy. He's heavyset and scraggly. Nice eyes. He sits down in front of me, ignoring my friend, ignoring everything but me.

"Can I help you?" I ask.

"Definitely." He smiles, a nice smile, but I can see from the way his eyes aren't completely focused that he's drunk. "Take me home with you."

I lean forward so my mouth is near his ear, aware of the way my hair falls over one eye. I smell soap and alcohol. He smiles.

"In your dreams," I whisper.

"Already been there," he says before he gets up and walks away.

I do take him home that night. And a few nights later, we wind up in bed again. We have sex, but I don't want to have a real relationship with him. This is new for me, keeping these two things separated, having the perspective to know I don't really want to date a drunk.

One night he says, "Marry me." He's drunk, which isn't a big surprise.

"Let's just stick to drunken sex," I say.

A few weeks later, I meet Michael. He lives with a boy I slept with during my summer of love, but this doesn't stop us from taking an interest in each other. I like his sharp intelligence, his sense of humor. I like the way his smile lights up his whole face, how, when I talk to him, he really listens. A group of us see the documentary *Buena Vista Social Club*, and after, recounting an emotional scene from the movie, Michael tears up. He leaves silly messages on my answering machine, pretending he's someone else. I like this guy. He's someone I could be friends with, someone I could see wanting to have around. When I'm with him, it feels different than it usually does. I don't feel like I'm jumping out of my skin when I'm next to him, like if he doesn't touch me I might die.

One afternoon, out in my car, I see him biking home. He follows me back to my place where we sit outside in the yard. I get us water, and we stretch out in the sun on lounge chairs.

"So you write," he says.

"I try."

"I was an English major," he says.

I turn to look at his light hair catching the sun. "You were?"

"Why does no one tell you not to be an English major?" he says. "Unless you go on for a doctorate, you've basically set yourself up for a career as a waiter."

I laugh. "No kidding."

"Guidance from parents might have been helpful too."

"What happened there?"

"I think my dad didn't have time for it," he says. "I have six brothers and sisters. Obviously my parents didn't know when to stop."

"Wow," I say. I pour him more water. "So your mother's a slut." I smile at him.

He laughs. "Actually, she's dead."

"Oh, my God." I cover my mouth. "Oh, God, I'm such an idiot. I'm so sorry."

"No worries," he says, still smiling. "She died when I was six. It was a long time ago."

"Sometimes I do stupid shit," I warn him.

He shrugs. "Don't we all."

A few days later, we go to a movie together, a real date, and talk for hours afterward over beer and wine. He tells me more about his family, and they sound so, well, normal, so completely different from my own family. When we get back to his house, he kisses me in the hallway. Soon, we're on his bed, stripping off clothes, but when he gets to my underwear I stop him.

"I don't want to have sex," I say. This is me talking, the same girl who usually can't wait to get a boy inside her, who's always looking for the moment when she can make a boy totally and utterly hers. Something important is happening here, and it isn't just that I'm not jumping to sex. I'm realizing love might look different for me than I thought it would. I don't have to feel all that craziness to be in love. Instead, I can feel like I do: calm, satisfied, and whole.

He smiles and pushes my hair back from my face. "Whatever you want," he says.

A month later, he tells me he loves me. Four months later, we move in together. Three months after that, we get engaged. This is what I've been waiting for, what I've been hoping for practically my whole life, and now that it's here I'm thrilled. But I'm also surprised to find that I'm scared

– terrified, actually. I'm still not sure I won't screw it all up somehow, but I try to trust myself for once. He spends time with his friends. I do the same with mine. I stay focused on my work. We enjoy each other's company, which is so different from all those times I sat with a boy, desperate for him to notice me. I give him the space to love me. I used to think I would get married when someone finally loved me enough to choose me. But this isn't about Michael being willing to love me any more than those other guys might have. This isn't a story about how some guy finally saves me from myself. I'm my own hero here; I do the saving.

One night, lying in bed together, I tell Michael the truth. I tell him about all the boys, about the desperation and running. About all that loss. I wait, afraid this will be it. He'll see me too clearly. He'll call everything off. But he just nods.

"I understand that," he says. He turns and holds me. I breathe in his familiar scent. "I think a lot of people probably do the same thing."

"But I'm also telling you something here," I say. "I'm not good at this."

"At what?"

"At this," I say. "At having a real relationship. I get jumpy and needy. I'm afraid I might freak out, do something stupid."

He holds me closer. "We'll be fine," he says.

"Do you hear what I'm saying?" I say, irritated now. "I may fuck up this whole thing."

"We'll be fine," he says again.

I try to pull away, but he holds me tight. "Why do you keep saying that?" I ask, still bothered.

"Because," he says. "It's what I believe."

◆ ◆ ◆

MY MOTHER OFFERS to take me shopping for my wedding dress, so I go to Chicago once again. I never thought I would be one of those brides, taken up with things like centerpieces and flowers and what font is on the invitations. I surprise myself a lot these days. My friends laugh at how obsessed I am. But I know how hard it was to get here. I deserve to have this fun. My mother and I visit Barneys' bridal shop and various specialty boutiques. I settle on a two-piece silk organza gown with stitching that looks like water rippling across. I turn around and around in the mirror. A bride.

In the airport heading home, I hug my mother.

"Thank you," I say. "The dress is perfect."

"It's a beautiful dress." She tears up. "I'm so glad you're allowing me to share this special time with you."

Her divorce is still fresh. This can't be easy for her. "I'm sorry," I say. "I know the timing isn't great."

"Yes, it is." She carefully wipes at a tear, not wanting to mess up her makeup. "We could all use a celebration."

I smile. I get it. This is her way of being genuinely happy for me.

At the wedding, she stands tall, her lips pursed. She finds a way to slip into her conversations that she's a doctor even when nobody's asked. She's horrified when Michael's and my friends call her Mrs. Cohen instead of the name she changed it to after the divorce, and instead of Doctor. This is hard for her, watching me move on, seeing my father with his girlfriend. Dad small-talks with her. He's jokey and fun, but also uncomfortable. Really, he's no different from the way he was when they were together.

"This is a great guy," Dad said on the phone soon after meeting Michael.

"I know," I said.

"He's thoughtful and considerate. What happened?"

"Ha ha," I said, but really I was annoyed. Did he think I wasn't worthy of someone like Michael?

"I'm just happy you found him," Dad said. "Now don't screw it up."

I had hung up feeling hurt, feeling old familiar things I had hoped I was done with. But seeing him at the wedding, seeing him scramble to make everyone happy, so insecure around my mother, I hear his words differently. He meant, "Don't wind up like me."

◆ ◆ ◆

Enough

NOT LONG AFTER the wedding, I go out with a few friends to watch a band. I sip at my wine and laugh with the friends. A boy in a booth on the other side of the bar catches my eye. Big eyes, long brown hair. He smiles at me, and I smile back. The band goes away, and so do my friends. I'm back there, the yearning, the hoping. Just me, my body, and this boy. After an hour, I decide I'd best leave. I stand to go, and I see him stand too. I make my way to the door, but he catches up to me.

"Hey," he says. "I'm Mark." He touches my arm, and my face grows hot. What have I done?

I bite my lip, embarrassed.

"We were watching each other, am I right?"

I grimace. "I'm sorry," I say. "I'm married."

Confusion crosses his face. And maybe a hint of rejection. "Oh."

"I'm sorry," I say again.

I get out of there fast.

At home, I change into pajamas and brush my teeth. Michael's already asleep, so I tiptoe into the room. For a moment I just watch him sleeping. I'm scared. I can admit that. I'm really, truly scared. I think of his words. *We'll be fine.* But now I'm not so sure. Maybe he doesn't get it. Maybe he thinks I'm not going to struggle anymore just because we're together. Or maybe he just plumb trusts me, which frightens me even more. I can't hurt him, not this time. Not when I've finally figured out how to accept being loved.

I climb into bed, and half-asleep he rolls toward me. He slips an arm around my middle and nuzzles his face into my neck. I close my eyes and listen to him breathing. How lovely that sound is. Maybe, I think, I don't have to be great at this; maybe I just have to be good enough.